William Arnold Stevens, Ezra Palmer Gould, Edwin Charles
Dargan

Commentary on the Epistle to the Colossians

William Arnold Stevens, Ezra Palmer Gould, Edwin Charles Dargan

Commentary on the Epistle to the Colossians

ISBN/EAN: 9783337379070

Printed in Europe, USA, Canada, Australia, Japan

Cover: Foto ©Lupo / pixelio.de

More available books at **www.hansebooks.com**

AN

AMERICAN COMMENTARY

ON THE

NEW TESTAMENT.

EDITED BY

ALVAH HOVEY, D.D., LL.D.

PHILADELPHIA.

AMERICAN BAPTIST PUBLICATION SOCIETY,

1420 CHESTNUT STREET.

ON THE

EPISTLE TO THE COLOSSIANS.

BY
EDWIN C. DARGAN, D. D.,
Pastor of Citadel Square Baptist Church, Charleston, South Carolina.

————————

PHILADELPHIA:
AMERICAN BAPTIST PUBLICATION SOCIETY,
1420 CHESTNUT STREET.

INTRODUCTION TO THE EPISTLE TO THE COLOSSIANS.

I. THE AUTHOR.

The opening words of the Epistle itself declare it to be the production of Paul, the great Apostle to the Gentiles. Is there any good reason to doubt this claim? None whatever; as will appear from the following considerations:

1. The external authority is ample and satisfactory. Schaff, in his "Church History" (latest edition, page 785), says: "The external testimonies are unanimous in favor of the Pauline authorship, and go as far back as Justin Martyr, Polycarp, Ignatius, and the heretical Marcion." Meyer ("Einleitung," section 3) puts it thus: "The external testimony for our Epistle is so ancient and continuous and universal (Marcion; Valentinus' School; Irenæus, "Adv. Haeret." 3, 14, 1 and 5, 14, 2; Muratorian Canon; Clement of Alexandria, "Strom." I. page 277; IV. page 499; V. page 576: VI. page 645; Tertullian, "De Praescrip. Haeret." 7, "De Ressur." 23; Origen, "Cont. Cels." 5, 8, etc.) that from this side a well-grounded doubt cannot be raised." We have then the statement of the Epistle itself confirmed by the unvarying testimony of ancient writers, and the unbroken tradition of history for centuries. This ought to be enough.

2. The objections from internal considerations have not been sustained. It is surely a daring thing to challenge, from internal considerations, the authorship of any writing which is as amply sustained as this is by external evidence. But German criticism, whatever else may be said of it, is at least daring; and so has ventured to challenge the Pauline authorship wholly from the character, contents, and style of the Epistle itself. These objections have been elaborately and satisfactorily answered by Olshausen and Meyer in their Introduction to the Epistle, and by Farrar in his "Life and Work of St. Paul." (Chapter XLVIII.) It is hardly worth while here to state and refute these objections. Those who feel interested may consult the authorities above referred to, and Schaff's "Church History," Vol. I, page 782, seq.

3. If Paul did not write it, who did? It must have been written by some one. Negative criticism wrestles in vain with the problem that itself has raised. As Farrar well says: "We might well be amazed if the first hundred years after the death of Christ produced a totally unknown writer who, assuming the name of Paul, treats the mystery which it was given him to reveal with a masterly power which the apostle himself rarely equaled, and most certainly never surpassed. Let any one study the remains of the Apostolic Fathers, and he may well be surprised at the facility with which writers of the Tübingen School, and their successors, assume the existence of Pauls who lived unheard of and died unknown, though they were intellectually and spiritually the equals if not the superiors of St. Paul himself?"

3

II. THE RECIPIENTS.

The Epistle is addressed "to the saints and faithful brethren in Christ which are at Colosse."

1. The town of Colosse was situated on the river Lycus, a tributary of the Macander. Its near neighbors were Laodicea and Hierapolis, some twelve miles away. Colosse was never so large or wealthy as either of the other cities. It is mentioned by Herodotus as a resting place for Xerxes' great invading host; and by Xenophon in his account of the expedition of Cyrus the Younger. These writers speak favorably of the city. But later on its two neighbors overshadowed it, and after the apostolic age it fell into a decline. It was visited by an earthquake probably near this time, and that catastrophe, from which its neighbors recovered, may have facilitated the decline of the least important of the three. Near its site, in the Middle Ages, a small village called Chonæ existed; but the actual ruins of Colosse have been identified only within recent times.

2. The church at Colosse does not seem to have been founded or even visited by Paul. We infer from his language in chapter 2 : 1, that he did not personally know most of the members either there or at Laodicea, though it is equally evident from other allusions that he knew some at both places. It appears reasonable to conclude from his language about Epaphras (1 : 7, 8 ; 4 : 12) that this "faithful minister" was the probable founder and pastor of the church. It may also not unreasonably be conjectured that Epaphras was himself a convert of Paul, and that the churches at Colosse, Laodicea, and Hierapolis were the outgrowth of the apostle's long and fruitful labors at Ephesus, the chief city of all this region. (See Acts 19 : 10, 26.) The church does not figure largely in subsequent history, though its neighbor Laodicea was one of the "Seven" addressed in Revelation. The Colossian Church probably declined in importance with the town, and was the least important of all the churches to which Paul addressed a letter.

III. DATE AND PLACE.

The Epistle was evidently written during a captivity of the apostle. (See Col. 4 : 10, 13, and Philem. 1, 23.) Which captivity was it? There are known to have been two of these, and a third is very reasonably supposed ; namely, (1) the captivity at Cesarea under Felix and Festus ; (2) the captivity at Rome, subsequent to the voyage and extending (Acts 28 : 30) over "two whole years"; (3) a second and later captivity at Rome terminated by his death, and during which he wrote the Pastoral Epistles. This, though not historically established, is generally accepted, as necessary to explain certain allusions in the later letters. No one holds that the letter to Colosse was written during this last confinement. The question lies, therefore, between the captivity at Cesarea and the first Roman captivity. Some of the ablest expositors, even Meyer, maintain that the letter was written from Cesarea. But the grounds for this opinion are very slender. Tradition unanimously designates Rome, and the allusions in Colossians and the other Epistles of this period strongly endorse this view. The case is well stated by Farrar. (Chapter XLVI.) The date, of course, cannot be exactly settled, but it was most likely about the year 60.

IV. DESIGN.

Although not known by face to the Colossian Church, Paul had a deep interest in them, as in all the churches. And this interest was evidently intensified by the coming of

Epaphras (1 : 7) with news concerning the character and dangers of the Colossian Church. It has also been suggested that Paul had learned something of the state of things at Colosse from Onesimus, the escaped slave of Philemon, who was probably a member of the Colossian Church. From these sources, then, Paul learned of a dangerous heresy, or tendency of thought, that was threatening the churches of this region—Laodicea, Hierapolis, and Colosse. He sympathized with Epaphras (1 : 9 ; 2 : 1 : 4 : 12, 13) in his deep concern for their welfare, especially in view of their present danger. Moved by this feeling, and no doubt at the earnest request of Epaphras, he writes this letter, together with one to Laodicea (4 : 16), to refute the incipient heresy and to set forth the truth of the gospel over against these threatening errors.

The general outlines of this error may be traced in the allusions of the Epistle itself, its more particular historical and philosophic affinities from what is known of certain sects and tendencies of the time. A study of the Epistle shows that there are two distinct elements of error which the apostle combats : (1) A Judaistic tendency—a regard for new moons and Sabbaths and holy days ; and (2) a Gnostic tendency—a would-be philosophic speculation about the unseen world, combined with ascetic practices. The question has been raised, whether these two lines of error were held by one, or two different parties. But it seems wholly unnecessary to assume the existence of two parties of errorists. It is better, with Meyer, Lightfoot, and other eminent scholars, to hold that we have in the views combatted by Paul a combination of Judaic and Gnostic elements. For it is impossible to separate clearly the lines of attack, supposing there were two distinct sets of wrong teachers. After warning them (in 2 : 8) against " philosophy and vain deceit " he proceeds to discuss the spiritual circumcision and the law of ordinances. And in 2 : 16, speaking of the fast days and new moons, he goes on at once, in verses 18 and 19, to allude to the empty speculations of the errorists. Thus it would seem to be plain that it was one set of false teachers, but that they held views at once Judaic and Gnostic.

Two explanations of this rather singular phenomenon are offered : (1) Lightfoot and Meyer (with others) hold that the views and practices of the Essenes, so far as they are known, presented just this combination of Judaism and Gnosticism, both in its speculative elements and its ascetic practices, which we find traced in the Epistle. (2) Franke, however, denies on various grounds the relation to the Essenes and explains the compound with the general statement that Judaism, especially in the Dispersion, had doubtless felt the influence of the incipient Gnosticism of the day. Either explanation *is an explanation*, but the able and learned discussions of Lightfoot give very great probability to his view. In either case, whether Essenes or not, these false teachers were by their wretched medley of Judaism and Gnosticism seriously endangering the purity of Christian teaching, if not the very existence of Christian churches, at Colosse, Hierapolis, and Laodicea. It was to meet and repel these teachers, therefore, that the letters to Colosse and Laodicea were written and directed (4 : 16) to be interchanged.

1. With regard to the form of Judaism opposed in the Epistle, not much need be said. It differed somewhat from that against which the Epistle to the Galatians had been directed, and to which allusion is made in Philippians. That was narrower, took more account of obedience to the law and submission to circumcision as necessary to salvation. There are allusions to the same things in Colossians, but the scope is broader. To show the similarity, or rather the sameness of the error, however, let Galatians and Colossians be compared : Gal. 5 : 2, 3, 6 ; 6 : 15 with Col. 2 : 11, with regard to circumcision ; Gal. 2 : 15-21 ; 3 : 1-14 with Col. 2 : 13, 14, with regard to the law ; Gal. 4 : 10 with Col. 2 :

16, with regard to feasts ; and finally, Gal. 3 : 28, with Col. 3 ; 11, with regard to exclusiveness. These passages compared will show both the sameness of the error and the wide difference in the treatment. If Lightfoot's theory about the Essenes be accepted, we might say, that in Galatians Paul combats Pharisaic Judaism ; in Colossians, Essenic Judaism.

2. Any elaborate discussion of Gnosticism is, of course, here impracticable. Three things, however, must be remarked : (1) That Gnosticism in the age immediately following the Apostolic, and even later, assumed great proportions ; became a wonderfully complete and developed system ; but that amid all these complexities and additions the simpler elements of an earlier stage of history may be traced.

(2) That there is very strong reason to believe that this earlier form of thought and speculation, afterward called Gnosticism, powerfully affected the Jews, whether particularly the Essenes, or the general body, about the time in which Colossians was written.

(3) That therefore we may expect to find in Colossians allusions only to the earliest stage, and yet to the fundamental principles, of Gnosticism. This is in fact the case.

What then was Gnosticism ? The word comes from the Greek for "knowledge" (γνῶσις). And so the term itself claims for the Gnostic, or "knowing one," that he has superior "knowledge" concerning things beyond the range of common observation and experience. We see traces of this claim in the allusions to the disturbers at Colosse in such passages as Col. 2 : 8, 18. 23. Besides the teaching that *all* should be instructed in the *knowledge* of the gospel, and similar expressions.

This superior "knowledge" occupied itself with two deep and difficult questions : (1) The mode of creation, and (2) the origin of evil. In its later forms Gnosticism had many a wild and fantastic doctrine on these matters. But even in the earliest traces of it noticed in our Epistle we can discover this leading thought. Paul opposes to all baseless and fantastical ideas of creation the great truth that in Christ all things were created and continue to exist (1 : 16, 17); that in him the fullness (πλήρωμα, "plenitude," a favorite word with the Gnostics) of the Divine Being dwells (2 : 9). The Gnostics held that matter was the seat of all evils, was itself an evil ; and this led them at first to those ascetic observances which are noticed and condemned in the latter part of the second chapter of our Epistle. Again, the Gnostic held to *emanations* from Deity which resulted in an order of things and beings, between God and man. To this idea allusion is made in the worshiping of angels and humility mentioned in 2 : 18.

We thus see that the design of the apostle in writing this letter was to refute the double form of heresy that lay in a dangerous compound of Judaism and the Gnostic speculations then arising.

V. CHARACTER AND CONTENTS.

1. The Epistle to the Colossians differs from the other writings of Paul both in style and matter, more closely resembling Ephesians than any other. Yet the thought and language are both in harmony with the other epistles, the differences being only such as would be natural to the same writer when writing under different circumstances, and for somewhat different purposes. There are in Colossians several passages where the language is rough and the meaning obscure. Dr. Hort conjectures that this is due to an early corruption of text. But this is unnecessary. The obscurity may be due to other causes. Others—"advanced critics"—infer that Paul did not write Colossians. But this

is, as Meyer says, "much too rash." Any man's style is likely to vary in different writings. And the likenesses to Paul's other writings are so great and numerous that they only serve to emphasize the differences. A forger would have been likely to produce a much more clever imitation, if he wished to succeed. But no forger could have expressed such thought as is here. The trick of style may be caught, but the live personality no man can steal. The great Apostle to the Gentiles lives and moves in every passage of this short but characteristic letter. It is vigorous in method, elevated in thought, profound in conception, clear in doctrine, warm in feeling—in a word, Paul's throughout.

2. The course of thought in the Epistle may be exhibited briefly, as follows :

I. (1 : 1, 2.) In the opening salutation he declares his apostolic authority, associates Timothy with him, and greets the church at Colosse with the Apostolic Benediction.

II. (1 : 3–8.) He expresses his gratitude to God, and his prayerful interest in them, because of the common treasure of the gospel which has been widely preached and is fruitful.

III. (1 : 9–23.) He more particularly states the burden of his prayer for them : (1) That they should grow in wisdom and grace. (2) That they should be thankful to God for his saving grace in Christ. And this leads him (3) to set forth the pre-eminent glory of Christ as the Image of God, the Firstborn, the creative Power, the Head of the Church, the Saviour ; and (4) to speak of their own reconciliation to God, and ultimate salvation by the gospel.

IV. (1 : 24–29.) He is glad to suffer in this cause, (1) even filling up any lack in Christ's sufferings, in (2) carrying on his work as minister of the mystery of God's will, and (3) while preaching and warning all to accept the salvation in Christ.

V. (2 : 1–7.) He tells of his deep interest in them and their brethren at Laodicea : (1) That the full blessing of the gospel knowledge might be theirs ; (2) that they might not be led astray ; (3) for though absent he rejoiced to be present with them in spirit ; and so (4) he earnestly exhorts them to hold fast to Christ as they had been taught.

VI. (2 : 8–23.) He is led now to warn them against the errors that he had heard were threatening them ; namely, worldly rudiments, and not the knowledge of Christ, in whom dwells the plenitude of divine excellence. This error appears in three forms : (1) Legalism, 11–17. (2) False philosophy, 18, 19. (3) Asceticism, 20–23.

VII. (3 : 1–17.) He now gives the true moral and spiritual principle, the antidote to all error in thought and practice, that is, heavenly-mindedness in Christ. And so he urges (1) the putting down of all low affections and wicked practices, and (2) the putting on of all elevated affections and good practices.

VIII. (3 : 18–4 : 1.) Domestic relations are then considered, and the morals of the home-life enforced in the appropriate duties of wives, husbands, children, fathers, servants, masters.

IX. (4 : 2–6.) Exhortation (1) to prayer in general, and particularly for himself in his work, and (2) to wisdom in demeanor toward those who are not believers.

X. (4 : 7–18.) Personal matters occupy the rest of the letter : (1) How they should hear of his affairs ; (2) salutations to and from different individuals ; (3) his autograph salutation at the close.

VI. TEXT.

The text of Colossians is in some places difficult to settle, and some interesting questions of text-criticism arise. It appears desirable to discuss them in foot notes under

the passages where the reading is doubtful, or incorrect in the text at the basis of the
Common Version. The writer can claim only a very rudimentary acquaintance with the
science of Text-Criticism, and offers here simply the results of his studies of such authorities as Westcott and Hort, Tischendorf (eighth edition), and the commentaries of Bishop
Lightfoot, and of Meyer as revised by Franke.

THE EPISTLE TO THE COLOSSIANS.

CHAPTER I.

PAUL, an apostle of Jesus Christ by the will of God, and Timotheus our brother,

2 To the saints and faithful brethren in Christ which are at Colosse: Grace be unto you, and peace, from God our Father and the Lord Jesus Christ.

3 We give thanks to God and the Father of our Lord Jesus Christ, praying always for you,

1 Paul, an apostle of Christ Jesus through the will 2 of God, and Timothy [1] our brother, [2]to the saints and faithful brethren in Christ who are at Colossæ: Grace to you and peace from God our Father.

3 We give thanks to [3]God the Father of our Lord

---

1 Gr. the brother......2 Or, to those that are at Colossæ, holy and faithful brethren in Christ......3 Or, God and the Father.

THE TITLE.—In the older manuscripts the title is given simply "To the Colosssians''; in some, however, it reads, "To the Colassians." No one regards the title as part of the original autograph. The better manuscripts give Colassians in the title, and Colossians in ver. 2. This is the form adopted by Westcott and Hort and Lightfoot, though Tischendorf and Meyer and Franke use Colossians in both places.

Ch. 1 : 1, 2. THE ADDRESS.

1. Paul, an apostle of Jesus Christ by the will of God, etc. In accordance with his established custom, the apostle begins by declaring his authority to speak for Christ. 'By the will of God'—not by men, nor by himself. It is a great claim that he invariably makes, and is not lightly to be passed by. **And Timotheus our brother.** Notice this association of Timothy (compare 2 Cor. 1 : 1; Phil. 1 : 1), who is not called "apostle," but 'our (the) brother.'

2. To the saints and faithful brethren in Christ. Or, since there is but one article, it may be read: 'To the holy and faithful brethren.' The point is of no great importance. They are called 'holy' or 'saints,' not because of any natural or acquired sanctity of their own, but because of God's saving mercy bestowed upon them in Christ. They were 'brethren in Christ,' 'faithful' in character,

'saints' by God's grace. **At Colosse.** Many manuscripts have the spelling "Colassae," but the best authorities favor the usual orthography, which is also that of the manuscripts of Herodotus and Xenophon in passages where the city is mentioned. It was a city of Phrygia on the river Lycus, a short distance (ten or twelve miles) above Laodicea. It receives complimentary notice from Xenophon in the "Anabasis." It is now in ruins, but there is a village called Chonos near the site. Little or nothing is known of the church at Colosse, beyond what the Epistle itself teaches. **Grace be unto you, and peace, from God our Father and the Lord Jesus Christ.**[1] This is the common salutation of the Epistles. 'Grace' is the favor, the blessing of God, especially in bestowing spiritual gifts; 'peace' is the peace of reconciliation with God, the abiding peace of a pardoned and justified soul. Compare Rom. 5 : 1.

3-5. THANKSGIVING.

3. We give thanks . . . praying. Apostolic example enforcing the precept of Phil. 4 : 6. Question whether 'always' goes with 'give thanks' (Lightfoot, Meyer), or with "praying" (Bengel, Olshausen, Ellicott). I prefer the latter. The 'always' need not be pressed to literal exactness, but should certainly not be weakened down to nothing, as a mere rhetorical flourish.[2]

---

[1] The Revised Version, with Tischendorf, Westcott and Hort, Lightfoot, Meyer-Franke, omits the words 'and our Lord Jesus Christ' from the benediction. Manuscripts favoring the omission are B D K L, 17, 39, 46, and others. Chrysostom and Origen both notice and comment on the omission as unusual with Paul. The manuscripts (even ℵ) which contain the addition were evidently manipulated by copyists to conform to the usual style. Clearly, therefore, the words should be omitted.

[2] A variation, unimportant as to the sense, but interesting to critics, occurs here. It is what Westcott and Hort call a "ternary variation"—that is, there are three readings to choose from. It comes after εὐχαριστοῦμεν ("we give thanks"); the question is, whether we should read, as in Received Text, (1) τῷ θεῷ καὶ πατρί ("to the God and Father"); or (2), τῷ θεῷ τῷ πατρί ; or (3), τῷ θεῷ πατρί ("to God the Father," without "and," both the latter having to be rendered into English in the same way). No critical edition (except Lachmann, I

9

4 Since we heard of your faith in Christ Jesus, and of the love *which ye have to all the saints*,
5 For the hope which is laid up for you in heaven, whereof ye heard before in the word of the truth of the gospel;
6 Which is come unto you, as *it is* in all the world; and bringeth forth fruit, as *it doth* also in you, since the day ye heard *of it*, and knew the grace of God in truth:

4 Jesus Christ, praying always for you, having heard of your faith in Christ Jesus, and of the love which
5 ye have toward all the saints, because of the hope which is laid up for you in the heavens, whereof ye heard before in the word of the truth of the gospel,
6 which is come unto you; even as it is also in all the world bearing fruit and increasing, as *it doth* in you also, since the day ye heard and knew the grace of

4. Since we heard—Revised Version, better, "having heard of your faith," etc. The 'having heard' is the temporal, not causal, use of the participle. The news came through Epaphras (ver. 7), and was not a matter of personal knowledge on Paul's part. The occasion of this thanksgiving was their faith in Christ and love for the brotherhood. Truly, a *sufficient ground* for thanksgiving always. Their faith was "centred in Christ" (Ellicott); "resting on Christ" (Meyer). **Which ye have** is found in the most important manuscripts, and is therefore inserted in the Revised Version without italics.[1] **To all the saints.** Their love was not confined to their own church and community of faith, but reached out to all who could truly be called 'saints.'

5. For the hope—Revised Version, "because of the hope"; probably better still, *on account of the hope.* This is not given as a second ground of thanksgiving, but as the reason of their love to all the saints, being the common tie of Christian brotherhood. **Which is laid up for you in heaven** (Revised Version, more correctly, "in the heavens")—that is, it awaits its complete fulfilment in heaven; also, the thought of its being safely kept may be involved. The hope is here in our hearts, but it also "entereth into that within the vail." Compare Rom. 8 : 24, 25. **Whereof ye heard before**—by the ministry of

Epaphras and probably others. 'Before'— *formerly, at first, before now.* Lightfoot's suggestion of an allusion in the word to the *later* teaching of the heretics as contrasted with the *earlier* pure teaching of Epaphras is possible, but rather forced. **In the word of the truth of the gospel.** Many expositors construe appositionally, "the word of the truth, which is the gospel"; but I think (with Meyer) that the thought is rather that the word is full of truth, and that the word of truth on this great topic is presented by the gospel. The gospel alone reveals the truth about this hope; the gospel alone makes it "sure and steadfast." This mention of the word of the gospel naturally leads to the next thought:

6. The Presence and Power of the Gospel.

6. Which is come unto you, as it is in all the world; and bringeth forth fruit. The best manuscripts omit 'and' before 'bringeth,' and add "and increasing."[2] Accordingly, we should read with the Revised Version, "which is come unto you: even as it is also in all the world, bearing fruit and increasing." The gospel is thus described as having come, and being now a *present reality,* among the Colossians, and is affirmed to be existing as a fruit-bearing and growing power in all the world. 'In all the world'—as a general statement, not as in

believe) adopts the second form, which is not very well supported, and may be left out. As between (1) and (3) the German scholars, Tischendorf, and Meyer-Franke, adopt (1) the common reading on the authority of א A C² D* E K L P; all cursives (Old Latin?), Vulgate, several Fathers. The English school, on the contrary, Tregelles followed by Westcott and Hort and Lightfoot, adopt (3) on the authority of B C*, some manuscripts of Old Latin, Memphitic, Syriac, Ethiopic, Arabic; Augustine and Cassiodorus. This, as the shorter and more unusual reading, is preferable, besides giving a reasonable explanation of the other two. 'On these grounds, it is more likely the correct reading, and has been accepted by the Revised Version.

[1] Here the words ἣν ἔχετε ("which ye have") are taken

into the text by Revised Version, Tischendorf, Meyer-Franke, on authority of א and most other manuscripts, versions, and Fathers. External authority is strongly in favor of it. But Westcott and Hort and Lightfoot put it in brackets because omitted by B, and being possibly a "conflate" reading. The point is doubtful, but it is most likely correct to insert with Tischendorf and Revised Version.

[2] Tischendorf, Westcott and Hort, Lightfoot, omit καὶ before ἐστί on vastly preponderant authority. It is retained by Meyer-Franke on grammatical grounds, though slenderly supported. Westcott and Hort, Lightfoot, Tischendorf, Meyer-Franke, insert καὶ αὐξανόμενον ("and increasing") on decisive manuscript and other authority.

7 As ye also learned of Epaphras our dear fellow servant, who is for you a faithful minister of Christ;
8 Who also declared unto us your love in the Spirit.
9 For this cause we also, since the day we heard it, do not cease to pray for you, and to desire that ye might be filled with the knowledge of his will in all wisdom and spiritual understanding;

7 God in truth; even as ye learned of Epaphras our beloved fellow-servant, who is a faithful minister of
8 Christ on [1] our behalf, who also declared unto us your love in the Spirit.
9 For this cause we also, since the day we heard it, do not cease to pray and make request for you, that ye may be filled with the knowledge of his will in all

1 Many ancient authorities read your.

every detail literally true. But even as a general statement, and including only the Roman Empire and contiguous countries, it is a very remarkable fact at that early date. As it doth also in you. The Revised Version is again decidedly preferable. He would not imply by saying that the gospel was bearing fruit and growing *in all the world* that it was not doing the same among them, and so at the expense of grammatical smoothness he brings in a second comparison to include them in the statement of the fruitage and growth of the gospel. Their advance had in fact been steady from the first. Since the day ye heard, and knew the grace of God in truth. Two questions arise here: (1) Does 'heard' govern 'grace' or 'gospel' understood? Does he mean to say, 'since ye heard (the gospel), and knew the grace'? This is Meyer's view. I prefer to follow the Revised Version, with Lightfoot. 'The grace of God' is the gist of the gospel; to hear and know one is to hear and know the other. (2) Does the phrase 'in truth' qualify the verb 'heard,' and thus indicate their true reception of the gospel; or does it belong with 'grace,' and so describe the truth of the gospel as distinguished from all errors? Alford combines the two: "In its truth and with true knowledge." This is not necessary. Either gives excellent sense. I prefer the construction with 'heard.' Meyer says: "It was a true knowledge, corresponding with the essence of the grace and the character of the gospel which had been preached to them, without Judaistic and other errors."

7, 8. EPAPHRAS. Two questions arise here: 1. Is this Epaphras the same person as Epaphroditus, mentioned in Phil. 2 : 25, seq., and 4 : 18? The name may be the same, Epaphras being a contraction, but it does not follow that

the person is the same. In fact, the greater probability is that there were two persons. The shorter form is always used in this Epistle, and also in Philem. 23, where the same person is referred to; the longer form is used just as exclusively for the other person; and then the localities and circumstances are very different. 2. Shall we read a faithful minister of Christ *for us,* or, *for you?* I prefer the former.[1] Epaphras is mentioned here and in 4 : 12, 13; also Philem. 23. From the notice in Philemon we mark him as a "fellow-prisoner" of the apostle, possibly from choice, in order to be with Paul, and learn from him. Here he appears as the first instructor of the Colossians in the gospel, while from 2 : 1 we infer that Paul had not seen the Colossians in person. Twice is he called, in a very commendatory way, a "minister of Christ." Paul not only endorses him as faithful, but even speaks of him (according to the most probable reading) as in some sort a substitute for himself. It appears that, being perplexed and troubled with regard to the serious errors of the churches at Colosse, Hierapolis, and Laodicea (4 : 13), he sought counsel from Paul at the cost of becoming a prisoner himself (Philem. 23), and that this Epistle and that to Laodicea (4 : 16) are the result of his communications.

8. Who also declared unto us your love in the Spirit—affectionate mention of his people by Epaphras. The phrase 'in the Spirit' denotes the sphere, and so the source and sustaining power of their love. It was a spiritual love, the Christian love, one of the "fruits of the Spirit" (Gal. 5 : 22), and possibly here having special reference to Paul himself as its object.

9-12 a. PRAYER FOR THE COLOSSIANS.

9. How naturally this follows! For this

1 It is very difficult to decide here whether to read ὑπὲρ ἡμῶν (" for us," "in our behalf"), with Lightfoot, Westcott and Hort, on authority of ℵ* A B D* F G, 3. 13. 33, 43, 52, 80, 91, 109, a g Ambrosiaster; or ὑπὲρ ὑμῶν (" for you," "on your behalf"), with Tischendorf, Meyer-Franke, on authority of ℵ° C Dᵇ E K L P, 17. 37, 47., and many others; d e f Vulgate, Gothic, Syriac, Coptic, and other Versions. On internal grounds, the reading of the English scholars and the Revised Version seems preferable. The reading is interesting as displaying a curious conflict between the best manuscripts and the versions.

10 That ye might walk worthy of the Lord unto all pleasing, being fruitful in every good work, and increasing in the knowledge of God ;
11 Strengthened with all might, according to his glorious power, unto all patience and longsuffering with joyfulness;

10 spiritual wisdom and understanding,to walk worthily of the Lord [1] unto all pleasing, bearing fruit in every good work, and increasing [2] in the knowledge of God; 11 [5]strengthened [4] with all power, according to the might of his glory, unto all [5] patience and long-suffering

1 Or. unto all pleasing, in every good work, bearing fruit and increasing, etc......2 Or. by......3 Gr. made powerful......4 Or, in.
5 Or, stedfastness.

cause. This, perhaps, refers to the whole preceding statement from ver. 4, but, naturally, has a more specific reference to the last turn of the sentence ; namely, their spiritual love, which awakened loving, prayerful interest on his part. **We also.** The 'also' "denotes the response of the apostle's personal feeling to the favorable character of the news." (Lightfoot.) **Since the day we heard it, do not cease to pray for you, and to desire.** See note on ver. 3. "To pray and make request for you," as it is more accurately given in the Revised Version. Both the praying and the making request are 'for them,' the latter term being introduced to amplify the statement and to specialize the subjects of petition. It would be still more nearly exact to render, "Do not cease on your behalf praying and asking." "He made mention of prayers in a general way in ver. 3, now he expresses what he prays for." (Bengel.) The noble burden of the prayer now follows. Compare Eph. 3 : 14-19. It embraces a number of particulars which glide naturally out of, and into, each other in the onward sweep of high spiritual emotion. **That ye might be filled with the knowledge** (apprehension) **of his will in all wisdom and spiritual understanding**—or, all spiritual wisdom and understanding. This arrangement of the sentence is better than that of the Common Version ; for the epithet 'spiritual' qualifies both 'wisdom' and 'understanding.' The exercise of our natural 'wisdom' and 'understanding,' under the control and direction of the Spirit acting on our spirits, is necessary to a real 'apprehension' of the will of God. This he prays that they may have. Compare Rom. 8 : 26-28. 'Knowledge,' here, is complete, thorough knowledge (ἐπίγνωσις), as distinguished from general knowledge (γνῶσις), perhaps used here in reference and opposition

to the false "knowledge" (or, gnosis) taught by the errorists at Colosse. 'Of his will,' either as (1) revelation, what he wills to make known, the 'mystery' of the gospel; or (2) command, what he wills for us to be and to do. Possibly both, as the second comes out of the first. 'Wisdom and understanding.' The first is a general term for the highest mental power, the second is used more especially as applying the first to the conduct. See Lightfoot.

10. Now comes the practical and outward manifestation of this high spiritual gift—**that ye might walk[1] worthy of the Lord unto all pleasing**, etc.—better, as Revised Version, "to walk worthily of the Lord," in a way suitable to the acceptance and exercise of the exalted gift of 'spiritual understanding' bestowed by the Lord. 'The Lord' here, as usual with Paul, is Christ. 'Unto all pleasing'—in such a manner as to please the Lord in all things; for he looks with pleasure upon the right use of his gracious gifts. **Being fruitful in every good work and increasing in** (or, growing by) **the knowledge of God.** Here is the outward and the inward improvement of the gift of 'spiritual understanding': to do all the good they can, and to know more and more, in order to do yet more good; or it may be also understood 'growing by the knowledge of God' as the means, rather than the sphere, of development. It is hard to decide, either being grammatically and theologically correct. Perhaps the usual rendering is more natural.

11. Strengthened with all might, etc. The verse would be more literally rendered : Empowered with all power, according to the might of his glory, unto all endurance and long-suffering with joy. This is another element of his prayer, a part of their spiritual development. 'Empowered with all power' refers

1 Westcott and Hort, Lightfoot, Tischendorf, Meyer-Franke, Revised Version omit ὑμᾶς, so as to read simply "to walk" (Revised Version), instead of "that ye might walk" (Common Version). The authorities are decisive for the omission. The Received Text has εἰς τὴν ἐπίγνωσιν on very slender authority ; Westcott and Hort, Tischendorf, Lightfoot, read τῇ ἐπιγνώσει with א A B C D* F G P, etc.

12 Giving thanks unto the Father, which hath made us meet to be partakers of the inheritance of the saints in light :
13 Who hath delivered us from the power of darkn·ss, and hath translated *us* into the kingdom of his dear Son :

12 ing with joy ; giving thanks unto the Father, who made [1] us meet to be partakers of the inherit-
13 ance of the saints in light ; who delivered us out of the power of darkness, and translated us

1 Some ancient authorities read *you.*

to the exercise of moral and spiritual power by those for whom he is praying; 'according to the might of his glory' gives the source and measure of their power. The word 'might' (κράτος) is used only of God's power; and here the divine 'might' manifests itself in their 'power.' 'Might of his glory'—not 'his glorious power,' but the 'might' which is an element and exhibition of that sum of the divine perfections which is expressed in the word 'glory.' 'Endurance' refers to the bearing of afflictions, persecutions, hardships in the path of Christian duty; 'longsuffering' denotes the state of mind toward those who bring these afflictions upon the sufferers; 'with joy' describes the temper with which the 'endurance and long suffering' were to be exercised. See Rom. 5 : 3. Some expositors (even Meyer and Ellicott) connect these words with the next verse, and read, "with joy giving thanks"; but Olshausen very correctly says: "'Giving thanks' itself alone conveys the idea of joyful resignation to God's will; but 'patience' and 'longsuffering' need the defining 'with joy,' in order to characterize them as genuinely Christian." The thought now naturally glides on without break into the matter of thanksgiving to God, which is a part of that worthy walk for which he prays on their behalf.

12, 13. GROUNDS OF THANKSGIVING TO GOD.

12. These are : that he has given us the hope of heaven, and that he has rescued us from the dominion of sin, and put us into the kingdom of Christ. **Which hath made us meet.** It is difficult to decide whether to read 'made *us* meet,' or 'made *you* meet.' I prefer 'us' on internal grounds, and on good documentary authority.[1] As to meaning, the thought

is plain, the words interesting. 'Made us meet'—that is, *fitted, qualified* us **to be partakers of the inheritance of the saints in light.** 'Inheritance' is not exactly correct. There are two words 'part of the lot.' Compare Acts 8 : 21. Olshausen says : "The saints conceived as a unity have a joint 'lot,' of which each individual has his 'part.' No doubt, as Lightfoot and Olshausen say, the turn of expression was suggested by the way in which the Tribes of Israel received the inheritance of Canaan. The phrase 'saints in light' may, and doutless does, refer primarily to the consummation of the glorious destiny of the saints; that is, to heaven. But it is to be noticed that it is contrasted with 'darkness' below, and is thus in some sort put in apposition with "kingdom of his dear Son," which the 'saint' enters by faith here on earth. Compare John 5 : 24. The commentators puzzle much over the connection of the words 'in light.' Meyer tries to prove that they go with 'made us meet,' as the instrument by which that meetness for the heavenly inheritance is effected. But this is decidedly strained. Nor is it correct to construe solely with 'the saints,' so as to say, 'the saints [who are] in light.' No doubt the proper connection is with the full phrase 'lot of the saints,' this 'lot' being characterized by 'light.' This 'light' may be that of knowledge, as opposed to the darkness of sinful ignorance; or, more likely, of *purity,* as opposed to the darkness of sinful depravity. The next verse brings out the contrast.

13. Who hath delivered us from the power of darkness, and hath translated us into the kingdom of his dear Son. Sin, wickedness, the influence and power of Satan, is darkness. 'Translated'—that is, *put us over*

---

1 Tischendorf reads ὑμᾶς (*you*) after the manuscripts ℵ B 4, 23. 80. 115; some manuscripts of the Vulgate, Ethiopic, and a few Fathers. Westcott and Hort also adopt this reading in their text, but not confidently, giving the other in the margin. Lightfoot adopts ἡμᾶς (*us*) in his text, but gives ὑμᾶς (*you*) in the margin, and expresses himself doubtfully in the note. Meyer-Franke prefers

the common reading ἡμᾶς (*us*) after A C D E F G K L P, most cursives, old Latin, some manuscripts of the Vulgate, Syriac, Coptic; Origen, Athanasius, and other Fathers. On internal grounds, the common reading seems preferable; but for the less pleasing reading to be supported both by ℵ and B makes a very strong argument for ὑμᾶς.

14 In whom we have redemption through his blood, even the forgiveness of sins: 15 Who is the image of the invisible God, the first-born of every creature:

14 into the kingdom of the Son of his love; in whom we have our redemption, the forgiveness of our sins: 15 who is the image of the invisible God, the firstborn

into the kingdom of Christ. Bengel aptly contrasts 'kingdom' with 'power': "Power detains *captives*, a kingdom nourishes joyful *subjects.*" The transaction is represented as past, 'translated,' not here in view of the decrees of God, as in Rom. 8 : 29, 30, but, as Meyer says, "through conversion to Christ, which is God's work." Yet there is, doubtless, here the idea of the consummation of this kingdom hereafter, toward which we look. We are no longer captives of the power of darkness, but are become subjects of the kingdom of light, which ever tends to its own consummation. 'His dear Son,' or "the Son of his love," as in the Revised Version; that is, the Son whom he loves, who is especially the object of the divine Father's love, and upon whose subjects also (John 16 : 27) the Father's love is bestowed. The notion of Augustine, adopted and defended by Olshausen, and even by Lightfoot, that the apostle here means to declare the eternal generation of the Son in the very essence and being of the Father, since God is Love (1 John 4 : 8, 16), seems utterly foreign to the connection. The more simple interpretation given above is held by Meyer, Ellicott, and others. By a very simple and easy transition, the apostle is now led on to speak of the work and glory of God's beloved Son.

14. The Work of Christ in Redemption.

In whom we have redemption through his blood, even the forgiveness of sins. The words 'through his blood' should be omitted.[1] Read: "In whom we have the redemption, the forgiveness of sins." It is a little smoother English to leave out the article before ' redemption,' as in the Common Version, but it does not mend matters to insert "our," as the Revised Version does. 'Redemption' is a leading gospel idea, a well-known Christian truth, and so has the article. The word literally means "a buying back," and is the act of securing release of an object or person by the payment of a ransom price. This 're-

demption,' or release secured by purchase, is represented as a present possession [' we have '], and so expresses the present state of the believer. This release is "from the wrath and punitive justice of God in its most comprehensive signification, whether specially ours or common to us and all mankind." (Ellicott.) 'Forgiveness' or 'remission' literally means "letting go," the act of letting go. The two words are here, and in Eph. 1 : 7, put together as fully expressing what we have through Christ. It is not that the words are synonymous, but that taken together they sum up the fullness of the blessing obtained for us by the self-sacrifice of Christ. The twin pillars of our hope in Christ—redemption and forgiveness !

15-20. The Glory and Pre-eminence of Christ. We have in these verses one of the most profound and important passages in all the writings of Paul. It should be carefully compared with those in Eph. 1 : 20-23 and Phil. 2 : 6-11. Using the thought of the redemption secured by Christ as a transition point, the apostle goes on to discuss the person, the glory, and the pre-eminent lordship of Christ. The style is elevated and vigorous, the language striking. The passage is not without its difficulties.

15. Who is the image of the invisible God. On the use of the present tense we may remark that it does not imply that at the time of writing, as distinguished from either past or future time, Christ was the image of God ; but it sets forth what is true of Christ at all times. Meyer thinks that while the notion of the personality of Christ in every manifestation is involved, the chief reference is to Christ in his pre-existent state. This is hardly necessary. The thought is a general one. Christ, the eternally pre-existing word, the humanly manifested Son, the now reigning Mediator, is, in all his characters, and at all times, the 'image of God.' Granting this much, we find no little difficulty in exactly interpreting the expression 'image of the invisible God.'

---

[1] Westcott and Hort give in their margin *ἔσχομεν* (*we had*), instead of *ἔχομεν* (*we have*), but on insufficient authority—B and some Versions. The clause, *διὰ τοῦ* αἵματος αὐτοῦ (*through his blood*), is justly omitted by all, on decisive authority, being clearly an interpolation from the similar passage in Eph. 1 : 7.

16 For by him were all things created, that are in heaven, and that are in earth, visible and invisible, whether *they be* thrones, or dominions, or principalities, or powers: all things were created by him, and for him:

16 of all creation; for in him were all things created, in the heavens and upon the earth, things visible and things invisible, whether thrones or dominions or principalities or powers; all things have been

So far as it describes the bodily manifestation of God in the human person of Christ during his earthly ministry, the meaning is clear, though profound. See John 1 : 14 and 1 Tim. 3 : 16. We should say that Christ was thus the visible and personal representative of God among men. But with regard to the pre-existent Word what are we to say? That in some sense, even before his earthly life, Christ was the outward (if such a word may be used) manifestation of the divine nature and person? It may be so. The creative Word is the 'image of the invisible God.' Then with regard to the present and future, are we to consider that to the angels and saints in glory Christ is the manifestation of the 'invisible God'? Here too is a more profound question than we can hope to answer. But whether the glorified body of Christ is the *only* visible manifestation of Deity in heaven or not, we are at least safe in saying that there, as here on earth, he will be such a manifestation. See what he says in reply to Philip. (John 14 : 9.) But let us not fail to note that the very difficulties which are raised by the term are such as to exalt our conceptions of the unspeakable dignity and glory of Christ, and that is the object the writer has in view. How much it means, to say of him that in all the relations of his being to other (especially human) beings, Christ is the likeness and the representation of the unseen God! **The firstborn of every creature.** (Revised Version, "all creation.") As to the rendering of the words (πάσης κτίσεως) for 'all creation,' or, 'every creature,' the commentators differ. Lightfoot prefers "all creation"; Meyer, "every creature." As the phrase is rendered in both ways, and either one gives here substantially the same sense, it is perhaps not possible to decide with positive conviction. I prefer the rendering 'all creation' as more smoothly fitting the connection. The real difficulty of the passage is in the title 'firstborn.' It does not mean either (1), that Christ is the first of all created beings—that is, himself being created; or (2), that 'all creation' is to be regarded as a *birth* from God, Christ occupying the first place. On the contrary, there is evident contrast between the ideas of

birth and *creation:* they are not convertible terms. Christ was *born*, the universe was *created*. Now, then, the expression means that he was 'born' *before* it was 'created.' He is the Son of God, 'Firstborn' and "Only begotten," before there was any "creation." So, therefore, in respect to "all creation" he occupies the relation of priority. From this it follows that over 'all creation' he occupies the relation of supremacy, such as is accorded to the 'firstborn,' and such as is pre-eminently due to the 'Firstborn' of God. [Is it not safer to say that Jesus Christ is here called 'firstborn of all creation,' because he is (of course in his higher nature) Maker and Head of all created being, representing and revealing in this way the perfections of the invisible God? That his position in respect to the creation is like that of a firstborn son and heir in respect to the inheritance over which he presides? Compare the language of Heb. 1 : 2, seq., with that of Ps. 89 : 27. "I too will make him the firstborn, highest of the kings of the earth," and with Ps. 2 : 6, 7, as interpreted by Acts 13 : 32, 33. This would agree with the next verse which appears to show why he is called 'firstborn of all creation,' and 'image of the invisible God.'—A. H.]

16. For by him were all things created, etc. In this and the next verse the superiority of Christ to all creation is further explained and developed. The translation of this verse in the Revised Version is far preferable, bringing out the delicate shades of meaning in the Greek more clearly than the Common Version. 'By him' (ἐν αὐτῷ) should rather be "in him." He is superior to all creation, because in fact 'in him were all things created.' He, in his presence, power, and energy, is the element or sphere *in which* the divine creative act took place. Excellent is Meyer's remark: "'In him,' a known classical indication of the dependence of a relation whose causality is contained in any one. . . . In Christ rested (causally) the creative act, so that it occurred not at all independently in a line of causes lying outside of him, but had in him its essentially conditioning ground." So in the spiritual kingdom, he is often spoken of as the element or sphere *in which* the saving power of God is manifest. The apostle goes on now to specialize the 'all things,' to emphasize the universality of Christ's creative superiority. **That are in heaven, and that are in earth.** Here the whole sum of creation is locally represented. But as if this were not enough, he proceeds to represent it in its relation to man's apprehension. **Things visible and invisible.** There is difference of opinion among expositors as to whether the descriptive terms 'visible,' or *seen*, and in 'earth' are to be taken as referring to one class of objects, and 'invisible,' or *unseen*, and 'in heaven' to another; or whether some things 'on earth' belong to the 'unseen,' and some things 'in heaven' (as the heavenly bodies) to the 'seen.' The question is of little importance. The apostle would say in most expressive language just 'all things,' of every kind and everywhere. And as if there might be still a lingering doubt as to unseen things, he adds: **Whether they be thrones, or dominions, or principalities, or powers.** These terms, no doubt, refer here and in the similar passages in Rom. 8: 38, and Eph. 1: 20, 21, to unseen creatures superior in power and knowledge to man; namely, the angels. No matter what might be their various orders and dignities, all of them were created in Christ, and so he stands superior to them all.

It would carry us too far to enter into a long discussion of the interesting questions brought up by these terms. In the learned notes of Lightfoot and Meyer, on the passage, full and sound information is to be found as to the use and meaning of the terms. The article by Kubel, in "Herzog's Encyclopædia," is very good; and Dr. A. H. Strong's discussion, in his "Systematic Theology," will repay careful study. Three questions, however, require to be briefly noticed: (1) Does Paul really teach the existence of angels of these various ranks and orders? On this point three opinions may be noted: (*a*) That he does not, but only used these titles as current in the Jewish, and especially the Gnostic angelology, to say that "no matter what you may call these higher powers, Christ is their Creator and therefore their superior. For this view there is a slight ground in the phrase "every name that is named" in the parallel passage in Eph. 1: 21. (*b*) That he does in these expressions

commit himself to endorsing, in so far, the angelology of the time, and therefore to teaching the existence of orders or ranks of angels to be designated and described by these terms, 'thrones' being the highest, next to God and so called, either because they are near and support the Throne of God, or because they themselves sit on thrones as approaching nearest to God in glory and dignity; next 'dominions,' or *lordships*, those who exercise power or lordship over the lower ones or men; then 'principalities,' or *princedoms*, those of princely dignity; and lastly, 'powers,' or *authorities*, those who exercise power or unseen authority in the lowest angelic order, just above men. (*c*) That he teaches the existence of those higher beings called elsewhere "angels," but that in describing them he simply uses for emphasis the current phrases, without meaning to divide the angels into orders, or to assert that these are really their correct designations, but only to say that there are beings to whom these terms are applied and Christ is superior to them all, being in fact their Creator. I incline to this last view.

(2) Whether we are to understand these designations to apply to the good angels only, or to both good and bad. In Eph. 6: 12, the terms "principalities and powers" are evidently used of the evil spirits. But it is not necessary to suppose that to be the case here. It may be supposed from that passage that those were "angels that kept not their first estate," but that many to whom these designations apply remained holy.

(3) Whether Paul does not intend to include also *earthly* 'powers and authorities' in this list, the terms referring both to 'earth' and 'visible,' as well as to 'heaven' and 'invisible.' No; it is better to understand the terms to refer simply to 'things invisible,' and interpret them as a further elucidation of that phrase 'things invisible, whether thrones,' etc.

Coming back to the main thought, the apostle now repeats it in somewhat different and very striking language: **All things were created by him, and for him.** In this statement are to be noticed: (1) 'All things.' After amplifying, he comes back to the simple statement, for after all 'all things' are 'all things'—no more can be said. (2) The change of tense. Observe the correct rendering of the Revised Version here, "have been

17 And he is before all things, and by him all things consist:
18 And he is the head of the body, the church: who is the beginning, the firstborn from the dead; that in all things he might have the preeminence.

17 created through him, and unto him; and he is before all things, and in him all things ¹consist.
18 And he is the head of the body, the church; who is the beginning, the firstborn from the dead; ²that

¹ That is, hold together......2 Or, that among all he might have.

created" instead of 'were created.' They 'were created' (aorist) as a historic fact, occurring once for all; they 'have been created' (perfect) and so continue to exist as a perpetual fact. (3) Use of prepositions. The universe was created, (a) 'in him,' denoting the sphere or element of the creative act; (b) 'through him,' as the instrumental personal channel of the creative energy; (c) 'for,' or 'unto him,' as the divine end and consummation with a view to which creative power was put forth. "The Eternal Word is the goal of the universe, as he is the starting point. It must end in unity, as it proceeded from unity, and the centre of this unity is Christ." (Lightfoot.) Elsewhere (Rom. 11:36; Heb. 2:10), such language can be referred only to God. Why here of Jesus Christ, if he were less than God? The thought goes on in power in the next statements.

17. And he is before all things, in time, and in rank. Note the use of the present tense, and of the emphatic 'he': 'He is.' Compare John 8:58. Lightfoot remarks, "One [the pronoun] emphasizes the personality, the other [present verb] declares the pre-existence." And by (properly in) him all things consist—that is, hold together, derive their perpetuity. "As the causal sphere of their continuing existence." (Ellicott.) "He is the principle of cohesion in the universe. He impresses upon creation that unity and solidarity which makes it a cosmos instead of a chaos." (Lightfoot.) He is not only Creator but Sustainer of all things. What grand language! How complete is the statement of the case!

18. In this verse the glory of Christ is shown in his relation to the church—And he is the head of the body, the church. 'He' is here again emphatic: he who is the Creator and Sustainer of the universe, even he is Head of the church. His headship of the church necessarily follows from his universal headship, and is made emphatic thereby. He is called 'Head of the church,' as giving to it existence, unity, and government, with special

reference commonly to the last. See ch. 1: 24; Eph. 1:22, seq. 'The body, the church, is, of course, apposition; 'the body which is the church.' Certainly not any one particular local organization of believers, but the general body of believers, called 'body' as being one living organism, though having many members, controlled and directed, unified and kept alive, by one Head, who is Christ. Not yet is the thought of his glorious supremacy fully expressed, and the apostle proceeds—who is the beginning, the firstborn from the dead. Franke in Meyer would restrict the reference in 'beginning' to the following 'from the dead,' and read thus: 'Who is the beginning—that is, firstborn—from the dead.' This is awkward and unnecessary. It is better to give the expression (with Calvin, Ellicott, Lightfoot, and others) a broader reference. He who is called in Rev. 3:14 "the beginning of the creation of God," is also the 'beginning' of the new creation represented in the church. Lightfoot well says: "The term [ἀρχή, origin, beginning] is here applied to the incarnate Christ in relation to the church, because it is applicable to the Eternal Word in relation to the universe." In the expression 'firstborn from the dead' quite a different sense is to be noticed in the term 'firstborn' from that which it has in ver. 15. Here the reference is not so much to precedence in rank as to precedence in time. Notice that it is not first born of the dead, but 'from,' or out of, the dead. He is the first of raised and glorified humanity. (1 Cor. 15:20; Heb. 2:11-16; Rom. 8:29.) Others had been raised before this, but only to die again. Enoch and Elijah, and perhaps Moses, had not died. In the sense of resurrection from death to life eternal, Christ was first of all, and so is pledge of all. (1 Cor. 15:20.) "His resurrection from the dead is his title to the headship of the church; for the 'power of his resurrection' (Phil. 3:10) is the life of the church." (Lightfoot.) Still the thought soars on, and we come to the expression that in all things he might have the preeminence. This is a vigorous rendering of the sense of

B

19 For it pleased *the Father* that in him should all fulness dwell;

19 in all things he might have the preeminence. For it was the good pleasure *of the Father* that in him

---

1 *Or, For the whole fulness of God was pleased to dwell in him.*

---

the Greek, and is retained by the Revised Version, though it is not literal. A literal translation could only be made at the expense of brevity, as thus: "That in all things he might become himself one who holds the first place." This sets forth his primacy in all things, from the dawn of creation to the resurrection day. The use of the verb 'become' (γίνεσθαι), rather than 'be' (εἶναι), is noticeable, for the distinction is everywhere maintained in the New Testament, as well as in the classical usage. The becoming first here is to be referred to the *completion* of his primacy, or, as Meyer and Lightfoot hold, to the "historical manifestation" of his primacy. "As he *is* first, with respect to the universe, so it was ordained that he should *become* first with respect to the church as well." (Lightfoot.) Or, more correctly, as he *is* really first in all things, so does he *become* first by that complete manifestation of his power and glory, the resurrection. This is, as it were, the crowning act, whereby he "comes into his own," whereby his primacy is fully settled and proclaimed. Some few commentators would restrict the meaning of 'all things' here to 'the dead,' and render: "that among all (that is, all who are raised from the dead) he might have the pre-eminence." This is grammatically admissible, and gives a good sense, but is not broad enough. The universal sweep of thought in all the context seems to forbid so narrow an interpretation.

19. Still carried along by the 'glowing thought of Christ's supremacy, the apostle makes next the profound statement of this verse: **For it pleased the Father that in him should all** (properly, *the*) **fulness dwell.** The 'for'—or, more correctly, *because* (ὅτι)—gives the reason for the foregoing. The indwelling fullness of God was the cause of his resurrection and pre-eminence. 'The Father,' or God, is to be supplied from the self-evident reference in 'it pleased.' In vain would it have pleased any being inferior to God for God's fullness to dwell in any one. This is so plain that it is not necessary to translate, "It pleased the fullness to dwell in him," which would be grammatically smoother. This

rendering is given in the margin of the Revised Version, and is preferred by Ellicott. But the main interest of the verse is not a question of grammar, but as to the meaning of the term 'fulness' in this connection. It occurs again in 2:9. The meaning is, all that which is filled up in God; that is, makes up the totality of the divine perfections, the completeness of the divine character. All that makes up God resides in Christ by God's own good pleasure. The careful discussions of Lightfoot and Meyer are worthy of thoughtful consideration. See also Thayer's "Lexicon of the New Testament." Particularly able and satisfactory is Lightfoot's discussion. ("Commentary on Colossians," p. 255.) He shows that the usual passive sense involved in the termination of the Greek word for 'fulness' (πλήρωμα) is here maintained when we take the *secondary* sense of the Greek verb (πληροῦν)—that is, "to fulfill," "to complete." The "fulness" (πλήρωμα) is, accordingly, that which is filled, fulfilled, completed; and so the complement, or plenitude, of the divine perfections. This disposes of the difficulty as to whether the word should be taken as active, *that which fills*, or passive, *that which is filled*; the sense seeming to require the former, the usage of the Greek the latter. But by considering the term to be derived from the verb in its secondary sense of "fulfill" or "complete," the passive sense is retained, and the meaning is as above explained. Another question is as to whether the use of this term 'fulness' (πλήρωμα) by the Gnostics influenced Paul in the use of it here. Baur and other hostile critics consider that the use of this Gnostic term indicates the un-Pauline authorship of the Epistle, inasmuch as the developed Gnostic use of it belonged to a later time. But both Meyer and Lightfoot have very satisfactorily disposed of this objection. For (1) it is easily supposable that the use of the word in the Gnostic systems of a later date had nothing whatever to do with Paul's use of it here, as the word was a good and intelligible one in itself, and very appropriate in the connection. Or (2) the more probable supposition is that, as the tendencies of thought which

20 And, having made peace through the blood of his cross, by him to reconcile all things unto himself; by him, *I say*, whether *they be* things in earth, or things in heaven.

20 should all the fulness dwell; and through him to reconcile all things ¹ unto ²himself, having made peace through the blood of his cross; through him *I say*, whether things upon the earth, or things in the

¹ Or, *into him*......² Or, *him*.

were later developed into the various Gnostic systems were now beginning to appear, so this term was already beginning to have with these thinkers a peculiar signification; and that the apostle very happily forestalls its later use by applying it here to Christ. The later Gnostics used this word *pleroma* to describe their conceptions of a great divine *totality*, from which various *emanations*, Christ himself being one, were at different periods derived. Now if this idea was beginning already, in a vague way, to take shape, how well might Paul say, that so far from Christ's being in any sense *derivative* from a divine *totality*, the totality of the divine perfections does, in fact, reside in him. We should not fail to observe the use of the word 'dwell' as of a permanent abode. It pleased God that his completeness should take up its abode in Christ.

And now, as the long sentence draws to a close, among his other glories the atoning work of Christ comes to view:

20. **And, having made peace through the blood of his cross, by him to reconcile all things to himself.** This brings home to the believer's own heart the great glory and power of his Saviour, who is the universal Reconciler. The passage is difficult, for though the general meaning is apparent, the suggestions are obscure, and the grammatical structure is uneven. 'Having made peace' is to be referred to God, as the implied subject of the sentence in the phrase 'it pleased.' He makes peace between rebellious man and himself. See 2 Cor. 5 : 20. 'To reconcile all things to himself.' In the Greek it is simply "to him," the pronoun not being reflexive. Yet it seems necessary to consider it as referring to God himself, though we should have expected 'himself,' instead of the simple "him," which *grammatically* would refer to the preceding 'by him,' meaning Christ. But to read: '*By* him to reconcile all things *to* him'—that is, Christ—would be awkward. To 'reconcile' is to "make completely other"

(ἀποκαταλλάσσω)—that is, to change the sentiments from enmity to love, from hostility to obedience. So we read in the passage already referred to (2 Cor. 5 : 19) that "God was in Christ reconciling the world unto himself." 'By the blood of his cross' is, of course, the blood shed upon the cross, and so in general the atoning death of Christ, its most significant feature, the shedding of blood, representing sacrifice in its wholeness. 'By him' is repeated for emphasis and clearness. The glorious Person through whose active energy creative power was put forth (ver. 10) is the same as he through whose atoning death the sin-estranged universe is reconciled to God. **Whether they be things in earth or things in heaven.** Bold language! Are we to understand the last clause as teaching that there are heavenly things or beings, as well as earthly, that need to be reconciled to God by the work of Christ? We cannot deny it. But it may be that the language is only employed to denote the completeness and universality of Christ's saving, reconciling work, as affecting the whole universe, being suggested by the large conceptions of the entire passage. It may be taken with a sort of understood hypothesis, somewhat like our Lord's remark about the "ninety and nine just persons that need no repentance." Yet it is not impossible that the language is to be taken literally. How, then, is it to be understood? Lightfoot and Ellicott decline to enter the boundless field of speculation opened by this language. The German writers, as usual, are bolder. Meyer rightly rejects as unscriptural the notion that the lost and fallen angels are so reconciled. But he holds that "the angels themselves, as all creatures, owe the restoration of their relation to God entirely to the mediation of Christ." He maintains "that our passage affirms that the *whole universe* is through Christ reconciled to God," and seeks to explain, as follows: Inasmuch as sin affects (1) total humanity; (2) even the inanimate cre-

¹ The second δὶ αὐτοῦ ("by him") is omitted by B and some other important authorities, and is therefore bracketed by Westcott and Hort. But it is most probably to be retained, as Lightfoot rightly judges.

21 And you, that were sometime alienated and enemies in *your* mind by wicked works, yet now hath he
reconciled.

22 In the body of his flesh through death, to present
you holy and unblameable and unreproveable in his
sight:

21 heavens. And you, being in time past alienated and
enemies in your mind in your evil works, yet now
22 ¹hath he reconciled in the body of his flesh through
death, to present you holy and without blemish and

---

¹ Some ancient authorities read *ye have been reconciled.*

---

ation (Rom. 8 : 19, seq.); (3) further also the fallen
angels who are under the wrath of God;
accordingly (4) the death of Christ removes
the curse of sin and points to the coming of
Christ to judgment, when sin shall be put
down and the harmony of all things be re-
stored. Franke, in commenting on this, justly
remarks that it is vague in the third and
fourth particulars, because it is already assumed that the holy angels have not sinned,
and that there is no restoration of the fallen.
Franke, therefore, goes further and maintains
that there are imperfect angels; that the holi-
ness of angels is not infinite; that God
"charges the angels with folly" (Job 4 : 18);
that there is an intimation (1 Cor. 6 : 3) of a judgment of the angels; and accordingly there is
reason to suppose that there are angels and
spiritual beings who need, in some sense, reconciliation to God; and that for these, as well
as for sinful man, the death of Christ avails.
It is, perhaps, better not to enter on so bold a
speculation, but, with the more sober interpreters, to say that, while the language hints
such things, we are not warranted in drawing
such large deductions. Yet it gives a grand
idea of the scope of Christ's atoning work, and
of the glory of the ultimate triumph of grace
in all things and everywhere.

21-23. CHRIST'S WORK IN THEM. Having
spoken of the power and glory of Christ in
this broad and striking way, Paul goes on now
to describe the application of that work to the
Colossians themselves.

21. And you—as a part of the 'all things'
on earth that are reconciled. The statement
is made of their former condition. **That were
alienated** (or, *estranged*)—that is, from God,
who is your proper Lord and Friend. **Ene-**

mies in your mind by wicked works—
that is, opposing God in the exercise of your
mind, your thinking powers exerted in opposition to God, and this mental enmity exhibited in 'wicked works.' Some (even Meyer)
interpret as if the enmity was on God's part
toward them, as if it meant "hated by God,"
instead of "hating God." But Lightfoot is
right in rejecting this representation as not in
accordance with the usual Scriptural language. The Scriptures represent God as hating sin, but not as *hating the sinner,* who is
indeed the object of wrath, but also of mercy
from God. **Yet now hath he reconciled.**
Some manuscripts have: "Ye were reconciled."¹ The grammatical smoothness is interrupted, as so often in Paul's writings, but
the sense is plain: "You, who were formerly
estranged from God and even hostile to him,
God hath now reconciled." The reconciling
act is commonly attributed to God. Compare
2 Cor. 5 : 18-20. The 'now' goes with the
past (aorist) tense because, though the act of
reconciliation is represented as having occurred in God's doing once for all, its effect
in those who were thus reconciled is a present
existing fact. Meyer and others quote a striking passage from Plato in illustration of this
unusual construction.

22. In the body of his flesh—that is, of
course, of Christ's flesh. Christ's human body
was the vehicle for the accomplishment of the
purposes of God's grace. Why the apostle
should have written 'body of his flesh' instead
of simply 'his body,' has given the commentators unnecessary trouble. Some (Olshausen
and others, after Bengel) say that it was to
distinguish the human body of Christ from
the church which is called his body shortly

---

¹ We have here a very interesting variation. Most of
the authorities read as the Received Text: ἀποκατήλλα-
ξεν ("he [hath] reconciled"), but B gives ἀποκτηλλάγητε
("ye were reconciled"), while other less important
authorities give variations from these. The choice lies
between these. Tischendorf, with the majority of the
authorities, retains the usual reading. Westcott and
Hort give B's rendering in the margin, though by re-

taining the common reading in their text they evidently prefer it. Both Lightfoot and Meyer-Franke
adopt the reading of B ("ye were reconciled"), and defend it with force. As the more difficult reading, and
explaining all the variations, it may be correct, and is
certainly entitled to notice as a probable alternative,
but not to be confidently adopted.

23 If ye continue in the faith grounded and settled, and be not moved away from the hope of the gospel, which ye have heard, *and* which was preached to every creature which is under heaven; whereof I Paul am made a minister;
24 Who now rejoice in my sufferings for you, and fill

23 unreproveable before him: if so be that ye continue in the faith, grounded and stedfast, and not moved away from the hope of the gospel which ye heard, which was preached in all creation under heaven; whereof I Paul was made a minister.
24 Now I rejoice in my sufferings for your sake, and

before. Others, that it was because of Docetic errors then beginning to arise! Meyer, that it was to emphasize the contrast between Christ's mediation and that ascribed by the errorists at Colosse to the angels who have no fleshly body! Others still, that it was so expressed as against the ascetic notions that the flesh was evil, for here Christ's fleshly body is represented as the vehicle of the atonement! All these things seem to me utterly unnecessary. It is just simply an emphatic way of saying a human body—a body subject to "the ills that flesh is heir to." No need to seek any deeper meaning, nor any need to condemn this simple explanation (as Meyer does) on the ground of tautology. The Scriptures, and almost all other writings, abound in such rhetorical emphasis. **Through death**—the means of reconciliation, and requiring a human, mortal body. On this doctrine, see the numerous similar passages, such as Rom. 8 : 3; Heb. 2 : 14-17, etc. **To present you holy and unblameable and unreproveable.** More accurately: "To present you holy and unblemished and unaccused before him." 'Holy'—as devoted to God, and therefore fit for his service; 'unblemished'—as the animals offered in sacrifice were required to be; 'unaccused'—as those against whom no successful accusation can be made before God as Judge. It is not certain whether this presentation 'before him' is to be regarded as referring to the judgments of the present life, or to that of the final day of accounts. If the reference is to the present life, it means that one object of reconciliation was to make the reconciled even now in God's sight 'holy, unblemished, and unaccused,' because even now that process is going on within them which will ultimately make them so in fact. There is something to be said for this view, and it is held by Lightfoot. But the reference to the Final Judgment is more in accordance with Paul's usage. See Rom. 14 : 10; 2 Cor. 5 : 10. This view is held by Meyer, and is, I think, preferable.

23. If ye continue in the faith. The rendering of the Revised Version is more exact: "If so be that ye continue in the faith."

The 'if' here does not imply doubt that they would continue, but expresses a simple supposition. Of course, the ultimate appearing before God without blame is conditioned on the continuance of that which establishes the blameless state. 'The faith.' It is a question whether this is to be considered as referring to their faith, and so to faith in general, as the mode of reception of the gospel; or whether it is here used in the less frequent sense of the object of faith, the things believed, the gospel itself. For this latter sense, see Gal. 1 : 23; 3 : 23, and Jude 3. Meyer insists on the usual sense, the faith of the believer. But the other view seems a little more natural here. In either sense 'faith' is the basis upon which they are to be **grounded and settled, and not moved away.** Compare 1 Cor. 15 : 58. The last expression perhaps refers to the efforts being made by the false teachers at Colosse to move them away from the true faith. **From the hope of the gospel**—for this also is a foundation. It is a sort of synonymous expression; the gospel is embodied and represented in the great hope it gives. **Which**—referring to 'gospel.' The remainder of the verse is more accurate as in the Revised Version. **Ye have heard**—which was preached (*heralded*) in all creation under heaven. This is not a fantastic exaggeration, as if he were stating an actual fact; but a phrase denoting the universality of the gospel according to its spirit and tendency, and the plain command of Christ. **Whereof I Paul am made** (better, *became*) **a minister.** This is not the word for servant which refers to the *Lord;* but that which refers to the *service* (διάκονος). It is used by Paul of himself and others in a general way. Sometimes especially applied to the office of *deacon*, to which it has given name.

24-29. THE APOSTLE'S SUFFERING, WORK, AND PURPOSE IN THE GOSPEL.—The mention of his having become a servant of the gospel naturally leads Paul to speak now of his labors in its behalf. This he does with great earnestness and force.

24. Who now rejoice in my sufferings. The best authorities omit 'who,' so that it is

up that which is behind of the afflictions of Christ in my flesh for his body's sake, which is the church:

best with the Revised Version to begin here a new paragraph: "Now I rejoice in my sufferings for your sake." 'Now' is not simply a particle of transition, of concession, but has, as usual when it begins a sentence, its strictly temporal meaning. It is not so easy to explain as a note of time. Meyer suggests that Paul says 'now' as distinguished from a former time when he was free and hard at work: "Now, though a prisoner and not as formerly free to go as I pleased, I rejoice," etc. Lightfoot conjectures that it refers to the apostle's spirits, as much as to say that there might have been a time when he was deeply troubled and disturbed by his trials, but now he rejoices in them. Neither of these explanations is satisfactory. It is not necessary to suppose that Paul was ever unduly depressed by his sufferings. Even in 2 Cor. he shows how he could at the same time feel their pressure, yet find in this occasion of joy. Nor is there reason to suppose that at this particular time he took any more cheering views of the grace of God than at others. So also there is not the least necessity to go back with Meyer to the former time of comparative freedom. It strikes me as being simply an emphatic 'now'—without special contrast with any former time, but emphasizing the present: Just now, at this very moment, I am rejoicing in my sufferings for you. 'In my sufferings.' These are the grounds of his joy—the things that gave him joy; not merely the untoward circumstances amid which, notwithstanding their untowardness, he could and did rejoice for other reasons, but rather the trials themselves gave him joy. This, however, not because they were sufferings, but 'sufferings on your behalf'—that is, for your benefit, for your spiritual good. As much as to say: Since my suffering brings good to you, I rejoice to suffer. 'For you'—as one member of 'the church, the body of Christ,' mentioned further on. 'And fill up'—present tense, expressive of a continuous and now realized effect of sufferings, both past and present; a view of an established fact which is thus a now existing and continuous process. And fill up that which is behind of the afflictions of Christ. There are several difficulties involved in this strong and unusual mode of expression, and they are of

fill up on my part that which is lacking of the afflictions of Christ in my flesh for his body's sake, moment. As was to have been expected, interpreters differ widely as to the exact meaning.

1. The word translated 'fill up' in the Common Version, and more fully "fill up on my part" in the Revised Version, requires notice. The word (ἀνταναπληρῶ) is a double compound, two prepositions (ἀντί, 'instead of' or 'over against,' and ἀνά, 'up') being placed before the simple verb "to fill." This is the only place in the New Testament where the word occurs. The usual form is the single compound (ἀναπληρῶ, "fill up"). The question is as to the force of the preposition (ἀντί, 'instead of' or 'over against'), which is here put before the more usual compound. The Common Version ignores it entirely, translating 'fill up' as if only the simpler and more usual word were here. The Revised Version tries to bring out its force by adding "on my part" —that is, "as compared with," "over against," Christ; but this commits the version to an interpretation of the meaning which is by no means certain. The only two reasonably satisfactory explanations of the unusual term, which must evidently have been used for a purpose, are those held by Meyer and Lightfoot respectively. The former explains the contrast expressed in "over against" (ἀντί), as involved in the ideas of lack and completion—over against a lack, I present you with a filling up. This is apparently the true explanation, but it is impossible to express it well in a translation. Lightfoot holds the rendering adopted by the Revised Version, putting the contrast in the persons, Christ and Paul.

2. What is meant by the 'afflictions of Christ'? The view taken of this phrase will help in deciding the meaning of the entire passage, and hence it is discussed first. (1) The natural and obvious meaning is the sufferings which Christ himself endured in his earthly life. Now of these, which? (a) The whole of his sufferings, including Gethsemane and the Cross; or (b) his general sufferings and trials, exclusive of his expiatory sufferings; or (c) his expiatory sufferings alone? (2) A meaning suggested to get rid of the difficulty; namely, that the sufferings here meant are those of the church, which is the body of Christ; and so her persecutions may

25 Whereof I am made a minister, according to the dispensation of God which is given to me for you, to fulfil the word of God;

25 which is the church; whereof I was made a minister, according to the [1]dispensation of God which was given me to you-ward, to fulfil the word of

1 Or, *stewardship.*

be called the 'afflictions of Christ,' the Head. (3) Another of the same sort, that by their 'afflictions' are meant the trials which Christ permits to come, or imposes upon his people. Of these (3) may be dismissed at once, as neither grammatically or contextually admissible; (2), though supported by great names (Calvin, Olshausen, even Ellicott, and others), is too fanciful, and too evidently manufactured to evade a difficulty. Recurring, therefore, to (1), we are still confronted with the question as to what phase of Christ's afflictions is meant. The notion that his expiatory sufferings *alone* are meant cannot be held, for reasons that will appear below. We are left then to choose between the views designated above as (a) and (b). It is hard to decide. We may say that (a) is more natural as the general, all-embracing description, while (b) (Meyer) would be more in accord with the well-known teaching of Paul with regard to the atonement; and also with his general use of words, for he never uses the word 'affliction' to describe the expiatory death of Christ. Perhaps the best way to put the matter would be to say that by the term 'afflictions' Paul means to describe the whole course of Christ's earthly sufferings, but without special reference to his death on the Cross. So we have the general view of Christ as a man enduring afflictions, not a special view of him as the sin-atoning sufferer.

3. If this be accepted as the correct view, what is then meant by 'that which is behind (literally, *lacks*, ὑστερήματα) of the afflictions of Christ'? In what sense were Christ's sufferings deficient? Certainly not in the sense that his atonement was incomplete, that his death was insufficient to atone for sin. This would put aside the whole New Testament view of the efficacy of the atonement, and contradict a prime element in Paul's own teaching. It simply means that Christ did not during the course of his human life experience every kind and phase of suffering for his people. He was not shipwrecked, he was not imprisoned, he did not have daily "the care of all the churches," and so on. There were some 'afflictions' that had to be borne and suffered

for the good of the church, which Christ did not actually in his human experience endure.

4. It thus becomes plain how Paul could 'fill up the lacks.' Not at all that he could by his sufferings add anything to the completeness and sufficiency of Christ's atoning passion, but that the Lord had left out of his own actual experience some things for Paul to suffer for the sake of those for whom he had himself died. This is no strange thought with the apostle. See Rom. 8: 17, and like passages. He here counts it a joy that his Master had left out of his own sorrows something for his servant to 'fill up' in service for the church. And this is explained in what follows. The interpretation here adopted is substantially that of both Meyer and Lightfoot, and is the only satisfactory one. For the other view, see Olshausen, Ellicott, Bengel.

In my flesh for his body's sake, which is the church. In my body, for his body's sake. Contrast between the seat of Paul's suffering, and Christ's mystical body, the mention of 'flesh' naturally suggesting 'body,' and this the figurative body of Christ. Of course, 'the church' is here taken in its broad sense as the general community of believers.

25. Whereof I am made (literally, *became*) a minister. See on ver. 23. According to the dispensation of God. The word translated 'dispensation,' sometimes "stewardship," literally means "house management," and is transferred into English as "economy." It sometimes refers to the personal management of the householder himself, and sometimes derivatively to the management of the house as entrusted by him to a servant. This last is the sense here. The apostle as a steward was entrusted with this part of the 'house management' of God. His work and service was that of a man charged with responsible office by the divine Householder whose 'house' is the church. Which is given to me for you. The office of steward is to be used for no personal ends, but for the advantage of the household, of which you at Colosse are part. To fulfil the word of God. This describes the nature of the task. It has reference to the *word* of God, and hence must be the com-

26 *Even* the mystery which hath been hid from ages and from generations, but now is made manifest to his saints:
27 To whom God would make known what *is* the riches of the glory of this mystery among the Gentiles; which is Christ in you, the hope of glory;
28 Whom we preach, warning every man, and teaching every man in all wisdom; that we may present every man perfect in Christ Jesus:

26 God, *even* the mystery which hath been hid [1] for ages and generations: but now hath it been manifested to his saints, to whom God was pleased to
27 make known what is the riches of the glory of this mystery among the Gentiles, which is Christ in
28 you, the hope of glory: whom we proclaim, admonishing every man and teaching every man in all wisdom, that we may present every man

---

[1] Gr. *from the ages and from the generations.*

munication of the truth of the gospel; and this communication must be full and complete. "To proclaim the word of God completely, in its whole meaning and extent." (Olshausen.)

26. Even the mystery — apposition to 'word of God.' A 'mystery' in classical usage was some secret that was made known to initiated persons, but kept from all others. Here, as usual in the New Testament, it refers to the hidden purpose of God in the gospel, which could not have become known without his revelation. Being revealed, it is no longer a 'mystery' in the sense of a secret or even a difficult thing, but only as a matter which required a revelation from God to make it known. **Which hath been hid from (the) ages and from (the) generations** Has the 'from' here its *privative*, or only a *temporal* force? Lightfoot says the latter, hidden from all times, that is, during and since all past times. But the proper privative force of the preposition seems to be required by the contrast in what follows: **but now it is made manifest to his saints.** What then is the meaning of the terms? The only difficulty is as to 'ages,' "generations" evidently meaning the men of all past times. With regard to 'ages' interpreters differ. Some hold that it refers to the angels! Others that it means the 'ages' from the beginning and so inclusively to the inhabitants of the ages; that is, all intelligent beings that existed before the creation of the world. Yet others (as Lightfoot) more simply say that it refers to the 'ages' of human history which are made up of many 'generations.' This is decidedly the preferable view, and we may take the phrase as describing all past time, and in its picturesque way emphasizing the fact that *never before* had God's purpose in the gospel been plainly and fully declared. ' But now is made manifest,' or *it was manifested;* a change of construction caused by the long sentence and for emphasis, as so

often in Paul's writings. 'To his saints'; that is, 'to believers in Christ. See 1 : 1.

27. To whom God would make known —rather "willed to make known," the word 'make known' (γνωρίζω) is different from that recorded above 'made manifest' and implies the communication of knowledge, rather than simply the exhibition of facts or truths. **What is the riches of the glory of this mystery among the Gentiles.** We may get at the thought better, perhaps, by a change of language: "What is the richness of the excellence of this revelation of grace as it is proclaimed, not to a select few, but far and wide to all nations." **Which is Christ in you the hope of glory.** Does 'which' refer to ' riches' as the grammatical rule would seem to require; or to 'mystery' as the leading thought and term of the whole passage. Either will give an excellent shade of meaning, leaving the general thought the same. It is better to take it as referring to 'mystery,' so that the thought would be: "And this revelation of grace is Christ in you," etc. It is ' Christ *in you*,' not *'among you,'* as it might be grammatically, but with a far tamer significance. This indwelling of Christ is of course by faith. See Eph. 3 : 17. Christ, in all that he means and represents, dwelling in you—personally apprehended—made your own. 'The hope of glory.' Beautiful figure. Christ in the soul *is* the hope of heaven. 'Glory' here refers, not to brilliant excellence in general, as in the preceding clause, but more especially to the consummated excellence of the future state, involving the bliss of heaven, the excellence of the saints, and the triumph of the Lord. Compare Heb. 2 : 10; 12 : 22, 23.

28. Whom we preach—better, "*proclaim*," as in the Revised Version; or, *publish, set forth by public speech.* **Warning every man** —a striking word in the Greek; literally it means "putting in mind" (νουθετεῖν), putting a man's mind on a thing by putting the thing in his mind. **Teaching every man—the**

29 Whereunto I also labour, striving according to his working, which worketh in me mightily.

29 perfect in Christ; whereunto I labour also, striving according to his working, which worketh in me 1 mightily.

1 Or, in power.

usual word for 'teach.' Meyer acutely observes, that the warning corresponds to repentance, the teaching to faith. Note the emphatic repetition of ' every man ' here and in the next clause. This sort of repetition is characteristic of Paul, as of other fervid writers and speakers. It gives here decided prominence to the thought that the higher Christian wisdom was not a ' mystery ' (in the strict sense) intended for a few initiates, but was a revelation of God's will; for 'every man' was to share in it, and every man's best development by it was the object of Paul's earnest endeavors. The repetition also gives us insight into the personal work of the apostle. Men must be preached to, not only in the mass, but singly. Compare Acts 20 : 31. In all wisdom—that is, in the exercise of all the tact, skill, prudence, knowledge, and grace that he could command for so delicate and noble a task. All is needed. Lightfoot interprets the phrase as applying to the subject of the apostolic instruction of every man ; that is, that he teaches the highest revealed wisdom to every man, as contrasted with those who kept higher subjects of speculation for the favored few. This is plausible, from the course of thought. But it seems more natural to refer it, with Meyer and others, to the wisdom exercised by the apostle in teaching. Ellicott tries, unsuccessfully, to combine both views. That, in order that; denoting the end in view. We may present—that is, before God as judge. See ver. 22. Every man. See above. Perfect, full-grown, fully instructed, complete. Compare Eph. 4 : 12, 13. In Christ Jesus; Christ is the sphere, and the only sphere in which such perfection is attainable. The best authorities and editions omit ' Jesus' and read simply ' present every man perfect in Christ.'

29. Whereunto—that is, for which purpose, the presenting of every man perfect in Christ Jesus. I labour—a word meaning to toil hard. Striving—a word involving the strenuous effort of a conflict, often used by Paul. According to his working. The striving of the apostle was not in human strength alone, but in proportion to and in accordance with

the divine energy. Meyer beautifully says: " So Paul points at last away from that which he himself does and suffers, to him in whose strength he does all, at once full of humility and exultant in victory." Which worketh. This power of Christ in him shows itself energetic. In me mightily — or, better, as in margin of Revised Version, "in power," showing both the place of its exhibition and the measure of its exercise. Vigorous, descriptive, intense language.

HOMILETICAL SUGGESTIONS.

Ver. 3-5 : The highest attainments of the Christian life, and those calling most loudly for devout thanksgiving to God, because of their being attained by his grace, are the fundamental principles of Christianity: faith in Christ and love for one another. So thanksgiving for the noblest gifts must have an undertone of prayer for their continuance, expansion, fruition. Ver. 4, 5 : Love because of hope. That which binds us to heaven should unite us to each other. A true Christian hope is more than a selfish longing. Ver. 5 : 'The word '— mode of communication ; 'of the truth '— basis of communication ; 'of the gospel '— fact of communication. Ver. 6 : 1. The presence of the gospel—in you and in the world. 2. The power of the gospel—bearing fruit (Gal. 5 : 22), and growing. 3. The purport of the gospel—the grace of God in truth. Ver. 11 : The measure and purpose of moral power. Ver. 12 : Qualified for the allotment of the saints: 1. Mentally, to comprehend its glories. 2. Spiritually, to share its blessings. Ver. 13 : 1. Contrasted conditions. 2. The power is of God. Ver. 15 : The glory of Christ : 1. With respect to God, he is his image. (Heb. 1 : 3.) 2. With respect to the universe, he is superior. (Heb. 1 : 6.) Ver. 16 : Christ's superiority : 1. To visible things. 2. To invisible things. Incidental but conclusive evidence of Paul's belief in the divinity of Christ. Ver. 17 : Christ the supporting power of the universe. The coherence of the universe is not due to blind " natural law," but to a regulating presence, a controlling power. Ver. 19 : Proof text of Christ's divinity : 1. This

CHAPTER II.

FOR I would that ye knew what great conflict I have for you, and for them at Laodicea, and for as many as have not seen my face in the flesh;

2 That their hearts might be comforted, being knit together in love, and unto all riches of the full assurance of understanding, to the acknowledgment of the mystery of God, and of the Father, and of Christ;

1 For I would have you know how greatly I strive for you, and for them at Laodicea, and for as many as have not seen my face in the flesh; that their hearts may be comforted, they being knit together in love, and unto all riches of the [1] full assurance of understanding, that they may know the mystery

1 Or, *fulness.*

---

fullness shown in limits even in his earthly life. 2. To be more fully known hereafter. (1 John 3:2) **Ver. 22:** The ultimate purpose of reconciliation, to present the believer before God: 1. Holy. 2. Unblemished. 3. Unaccused. **Ver. 23:** Three reasons for holding fast the gospel: 1. They had heard it in its simplicity from Epaphras. 2. It is the universal hope-bringing revelation from God. 3. It is ministered by the apostle himself. **Ver. 24:** Body for body: 1. Paul's body a means of suffering. 2. Christ's body (the church) to be benefited thereby. **Ver. 25:** The ministry a stewardship: 1. Entrusted by the Head of the household. 2. Exercised for the benefit of the household. **Ver. 26:** In God's time, what had been a mystery becomes a revelation. **Ver. 27:** 1. The excellence of the gospel—gloriously rich. 2. The extent of the gospel—not for Jews alone, but for all. (1) 'Christ in you'—by faith, love, obedience. (2) 'The hope of glory'—of personal excellence, blissful surroundings, triumphant truth. **Ver. 28:** 1. Scope of preaching—warning and teaching. 2. Purpose of preaching—Christly perfection of the believer.

Ch. 2: 1-5. PAUL'S PERSONAL INTEREST IN THE COLOSSIANS.

1. For I would that ye knew—better, the Revised Version, "For I would have you know"; but better still, and more literal, '*For I wish you to know.*' The 'for' goes back to 1 : 29, especially to 'striving.' **Conflict,** here, is the noun from which the verb 'to strive' is made. So the reference of this 'for' would be plainer if we should read 1 : 29, in connection with this verse: 'I toil striving . . . for I want you to know how great a strife I have.' The Revised Version, by a slight change of construction, brings out the

sense very well. **For you**—for your benefit, on your behalf.[1] The 'conflict' or 'striving' is, as just stated, that referred to in 1 : 29; or it may, though suggested by the foregoing phrase, have special reference to his intense concern in prayer for their good. (4:12.) **And for them at Laodicea.** See 4 : 13, 16. Laodicea was a city in the same region of country as Colosse. The church there was exposed to the same dangers as the Colossian Church, and was similarly addressed by letter. **And as many as have not seen my face in the flesh.** This is not perfectly clear. 1. It may mean that the Christians at Colosse and Laodicea, like others, had not seen his face; but this did not hinder his earnest concern for their spiritual welfare. 2. Or it may be that only those in Laodicea had not seen him, but for them and others like them, as well as for his personal acquaintances, he felt this interest. 3. Or that even for those who (*not* like the brethren at Colosse and Laodicea, who knew him) had never seen him at all, he felt this concern, and how much more for them. Of these, both on grammatical and contextual grounds, I prefer the first, because the following expression "*their* hearts" would more naturally include all three of the cases mentioned—'you,' 'them at Laodicea,' and 'us many as have not seen.' His concern was for all whom he could help, and whom he knew of through others, even though he was not personally acquainted with them.

2. That their hearts might (better, *may*) **be comforted.** 'That' is here *in order that,* expressing the purpose of his earnest concern for them. 'Comforted' is hardly "confirmed, strengthened" (Lightfoot), but should rather retain its usual significance. Amid the perils and trials of the time they needed just such comfort as the assurance of an apostle's earnest prayers for them would

---

[1] Question, whether to read περί ("concerning," "about"), or ὑπέρ ("for," "in behalf of"). The latter better attested and adopted by Westcott and Hort, Tischendorf, and Lightfoot.

bring, and this comfort received by them would be manifest in their being united in love. **Being knit together in love** (better, as the Revised Version,[1] "they being knit.") The construction changes, as by 'their hearts' he really meant *themselves*. This phrase, 'they being knit together in love,' is a strong and striking expression for complete union in Christian love. It is descriptive of the comfort they were to have. How it increases comfort for those who have a common need of it to be united in love! **In love**—as the element in which their union occurs; **unto all riches,** etc.—as the purpose or end in view, or result to be reached by their being thus consolingly knit together. **Of the full assurance of understanding** (or, *completeness* of understanding). A full assurance of divine truth by understanding it is indeed a rich possession. **To the acknowledgment of the mystery.** Read with the Revised Version, "that they may know the mystery," which, though a change in the construction, brings out the sense. 'Acknowledgment' is a wholly wrong translation, and suggests an idea entirely foreign to the passage. It is a surprising mistake in the King James translators in which they departed from the earlier English versions, being prob-

ably misled by the Vulgate *in agnitionem*, or *acknowledgment*. The Greek word (ἐπίγνωσις) means rather "comprehension," "complete knowing," "full knowledge." The thought is that their full understanding might rise to a clear comprehension of 'the mystery' (or, *revealed will*) of God. One passage, quoted by Liddell and Scott, gives the word the meaning of "acknowledgment," but this is rare in classical Greek, and it never has that meaning in the New Testament. The Vulgate rendering is ambiguous, and so misled the Revisers of 1611. On 'mystery,' see note on 1 : 26. **Of God, and of the Father, and of Christ.** The text is here very uncertain.[2] The most probably correct text is simply 'Of God, of Christ.' A question as to the meaning then arises. Three constructions have been proposed: 1. "Of the God of Christ" —that is, the 'mystery' revealed by the God whom Christ represents and makes known. This is Meyer's interpretation. It is harsh and unnatural, and not supported by usage. 2. "Of God, that is, Christ," so taking "Christ" as in apposition with "God." This is grammatical and is theologically correct, but it is not in accord with Paul's usual style, and is not so conformable to the context as the following. 3. "Of God, even Christ."

---

[1] Westcott and Hort, Tischendorf, Lightfoot, Meyer-Franke, all read συμβιβασθέντες (Revised Version, "*they* being knit together," referring to the persons), and not συμβιβασθέντων ("being knit together," referring to their hearts), after the best authorities, ℵ* A B C, etc.

[2] One of the most interesting and important textual difficulties in this Epistle, and indeed in the whole New Testament, meets us here. It lies in the words following μυστηρίου ('mystery'). Lightfoot enumerates fully eleven variations! Thus the authorities are apparently hopelessly divided; and it would seem impossible to form a decided opinion. Here are the readings:

1. τοῦ θεοῦ, χριστοῦ ("of God, Christ"). B, Hilary of Poitiers, Tischendorf, Lightfoot, Meyer-Franke, Westcott and Hort (though Hort doubtfully).

2. τοῦ θεοῦ ὅ ἐστιν χριστός ("of God, which [that is, the' mystery'] is Christ"). D, d, e, Vigilius, Augustine.

3. τοῦ θεοῦ ἐν χριστῷ ("of God in Christ"), 17. (with τοῦ also before ἐν). Clement of Alexandria, twice, and, with some minor variations, Ambrosiaster, Armenian Version.

4. τοῦ θεοῦ ("of God"). D² P 37. 67,² 71. 80. 116.

5. τοῦ θεοῦ πατρὸς χριστοῦ ("of God the Father of Christ"). ℵ* A C 4. (A C t. τοῦ before χρ.) Memphitic, Thebaic, Arabic, some manuscripts of the Vulgate.

6. τοῦ θεοῦ καὶ πατρὸς τοῦ χριστοῦ ("of the God and Father of Christ"). ℵᶜ and a corrector in the Harclean Syriac.

7. τοῦ θεοῦ πατρὸς καὶ τοῦ χριστοῦ ("of God the Father and of Christ"). 47. 73. Peshito, some Fathers, with variations.

8. τοῦ θεοῦ καὶ πατρὸς καὶ τοῦ χριστοῦ ("of God and of the Father and of Christ"). D³ K L, most cursives, Harclean Syriac (text), Theodoret, and other Fathers.

These are the most important variations. It will seem pretty clear on examination that all of these, except the third, are attempts to explain the difficulty in the first, and that they are therefore really so many testimonies to the genuineness of the first and the purity of B. This is the view taken by Lightfoot, Meyer-Franke, Westcott and (apparently) Tischendorf. It appears, on the whole, most probable. Hort, however, not seeing how the second could be derived from the first, thinks that its existence, though so slenderly supported, throws doubt on the genuineness of the first, and he seems inclined to read, conjecturally, τοῦ ἐν χριστῷ ("which is in Christ"), as giving an explanation both of the first and second. This is very precarious; and it appears pretty conclusively that the first must be accepted. This the Revisers have done.

.

3 In whom are hid all the treasures of wisdom and knowledge.
4 And this I say, lest any man should beguile you with enticing words.
5 For though I be absent in the flesh, yet am I with you in the spirit, joying and beholding your order, and the steadfastness of your faith in Christ.
6 As ye have therefore received Christ Jesus the Lord, so walk ye in him:

3 tery of God, *even* Christ, in whom are all the
4 treasures of wisdom and knowledge hidden. This I say, that no one may delude you with per-
5 suasiveness of speech. For though I am absent in the flesh, yet am I with you in the spirit, joying and beholding your order, and the stedfastness of your faith in Christ.
6 As therefore ye received Christ Jesus the Lord,

1 The ancient authorities vary much in the text of this passage.

This puts "Christ" in apposition with "mystery," the mystery of God, which mystery is Christ. This is also grammatically correct, suits the context well, resembles the modes of expression in 1 : 27 and in 1 Tim. 3 : 16, and so is decidedly preferable to the other two. See the excellent notes of Ellicott and Lightfoot, both of whom adopt and defend this view.

3. In whom (in Christ) are hid, etc. Better read, as in the Revised Version, "In whom are all the treasures . . . hidden." These treasures are 'in him,' and they are 'hidden.' Yet this does not mean that they are hidden in the sense of concealed, or destined to concealment, but rather as *laid up, stored away*, waiting to be revealed when God shall see fit. Compare 1 Cor. 1 : 7. These treasures are hidden from the unspiritual and self-sufficient. But they are in Christ for all who will come to him. It is possible that Lightfoot's ingenious suggestion of a reference here to the "hidden wisdom" of the false teachers may be correct. They prided themselves on having a higher wisdom, which was kept hidden from the common herd and made known only to the favored few. So it is as if Paul would say: "Your false teachers speak of hidden wisdom for the initiated only, but I say that in Christ are all the treasures of wisdom and knowledge; they are 'hidden' indeed from those who refuse him, but richly stored up for any and all who accept him as Lord; 'hidden' in part even from these, but being ever more and more revealed, until the full revelation shall come." Wisdom and knowledge here are, of course, not the divine attributes, but the objects of human attainment. There are stored up in Christ rich treasures of divine truth which it is true knowledge to acquire, the best wisdom to apply.

4. And this I say—referring to what is contained in ver. 1–3: "(1) The declaration

that all knowledge is comprehended in Christ; (2) the expression of his own personal anxiety that they should remain steadfast in this conviction. This last point explains the language that follows." (Lightfoot.) Lest any man (or, *that no one¹*) may beguile you—reason you away from your convictions, a word often used in classical Greek. With enticing words (or, *persuasiveness of speech*)—with plausible arguments, as the false teachers were then trying to do.

5. For though I be absent. See ver. 1. With you in the spirit—that is, in thought, heart, and concern; there is no reference to the Holy Spirit. Joying and beholding—that is, rejoicing to see. This seems to be the simplest way to construe the rather unusual arrangement. Ellicott and Meyer discuss the matter elaborately, but, after all, not very satisfactorily. Your order—that is, your orderliness in walk and behavior. And the steadfastness of your faith in Christ (rather, *the solid foundation of your faith*). As Ellicott remarks, it is agreeable to know that the Colossians, though tried by false teachers, were substantially sound in faith. Some (as Lightfoot) take the words in a military sense, 'order' or "array" as of an army drawn up in line, and 'solidness' as of a phalanx or legion, solidly opposed to the enemy. The reference is possible, but hardly natural, in this connection, and rather fanciful.

6, 7. A GENERAL EXHORTATION.

6. As ye have therefore received. Better omit 'have'; the tense is not the perfect, but the past indefinite. Christ Jesus the Lord. Note that it is not merely abstract truth that they received, but the personal 'Christ Jesus.' It is, as Meyer observes, a solemn statement of the essential principle of the faith they received, the Christ, that is Jesus, in his office and character as Lord. Following out this last thought comes the command. So walk

¹ Read μηδείς (" no one "), instead of μή τις (" lest any one "), with Tischendorf, Westcott and Hort, Lightfoot, Meyer-Franke following all the better authorities.

7 Rooted and built up in him, and stablished in the faith, as ye have been taught, abounding therein with thanksgiving.

8 Beware lest any man spoil you through philosophy and vain deceit, after the tradition of men, after the rudiments of the world, and not after Christ.

7 *so* walk in him, rooted and builded up in him, and stablished [1] in your faith, even as ye were taught, abounding [2] in thanksgiving.

8 [3] Take heed lest there shall be any one that maketh spoil of you through his philosophy and vain deceit, after the tradition of men, after the

1 Or, *by*......2 Some ancient authorities insert *in it*......3 Or, *See whether*.

ye in him. The 'walk' is a common Bible phrase for the 'conduct,' or the 'manner of life.' Here it is the same as saying, "Live in accordance with the principles you received when you accepted Christ as Saviour and Lord."

7. Rooted and built up in him. He defines more particularly the characteristics of this walk: 'Rooted in him,' as the soil in which the tree is planted and by which it grows. 'Built up in him,' as the foundation upon which the superstructure of a just character is reared. Stablished in the faith—or, more probably *confirmed by faith*, as the medium of connection with Christ. Abounding therein with thanksgiving—or, *abounding in thanksgiving*,[1] as the suitable frame of mind for one who enjoys such blessings. Observe the change back and forth of the tenses of these participles. 'Rooted' is perfect, describing a fact accomplished in the past when they took Christ for their Lord, but in its results still abiding; 'built up,' or rather *being built*, is present, describing a continuous process going on as a consequence of the other; 'confirmed' is perfect, again taking the mind back to the past act of faith, resulting, however, still in their firm stand; 'abounding' is present, again pointing to what should be a continuous and habitual state of mind. Observe, too, the rapid change of metaphors: rooted, built, confirmed, all giving vividness and fullness to the description of this state in Christ. As ye have been (better, *were*) taught—that is, by Epaphras. (1:7.)

8-23. Special Warning against the False Teachings at Colosse.—The main difficulties, as well as the leading interest of the Epistle, centre in this passage. For the nature of the false teachings at Colosse, see the "Introduction," and more especially the careful discussions of Lightfoot and Meyer. The

three leading errors combated in the passage appear to be: (1) A false philosophy; (2) a burdensome ceremonialism; (3) a rigid and worthless asceticism, all leading away from Christ.

8. Beware lest any man spoil you. The warning begins in general terms. 'Spoil you:' This is not in the sense of "corrupt" you, which the Greek does not have at all, and is only an ambiguity of the English translation; nor in the sense of "despoil," "rob" you; but is more literally given in the Revised Version, "make spoil of you." The Greek is very vigorous and definite, presenting to the mind the picture of a person dragging away another as his booty. The form of the Greek (future indicative), which is clearly, albeit a little clumsily, expressed in the Revised Version, shows that it was a real and not simply a supposable danger which the apostle has in mind. Though the indefinite mode of expression, 'any one' (τις), is used, a definite set of persons, or possibly one person, is clearly in view. Compare our own use of the expression, "a certain person." Somewhat as if he would say: "Take heed; it looks as if somebody were going to drag you away as spoil."

Through philosophy and vain deceit—that is, what passed for philosophy and was empty delusion. Taking the fair name of philosophy, it was really deception, empty of all good, and unable to satisfy mind or heart. The particular form of so-called 'philosophy' to which the Colossians were exposed was a theosophic speculation, in which the follies of the later Gnosticism were already beginning to appear. (See "Introduction.") All the Commentators remark that the absence of both article and preposition before 'vain deceit' in the Greek shows that this is not a separate idea, but a characterization of the 'philosophy.' This is of course not philosophy in

1 More literally, *abounding in it, in thanksgiving*. The reading is uncertain. If the 'in it' be retained, the reference is of course to faith, in which they must abound with a thankful heart to God for this gift. (Eph. 2:8.) If the 'in it' be omitted, we read, as in the

Revised Version, "abounding in thanksgiving" as the quality which should characterize their whole state of heart and mind in the reception and exercise of the gospel gifts.

9 For in him dwelleth all the fulness of the Godhead bodily.
10 And ye are complete in him, which is the head of all principality and power:

9 [1] rudiments of the world, and not after Christ: for in him dwelleth all the fulness of the Godhead 10 bodily, and in him ye are made full, who is the

1 Or, *elements*.

our modern sense of the word, nor even as currently understood then, but (as indicated by the article in Greek) that particular form of teaching to which the Colossians were then exposed, and which doubtless called itself 'philosophy.' **After the traditions of man.** The character of the philosophy and vain deceit. It was of purely human origin, being simply handed down from man to man. There is perhaps allusion here to the Kabbala, the mystic traditions of Judaism, with which the false teaching at Colosse had some affinity. The form of the sentence is interesting. This teaching is: (1) positively; (*a*) of human origin; (*b*) of earthly nature; (2) negatively, not Christian. **After the rudiments of the world.** 'Rudiments' are "elements" or "first principles" or "a b c." The very first principles of this rapacious philosophy are of the earth earthy. This is the simplest interpretation. The notion of some of the Fathers that by the Greek term (στοιχεία) is meant not 'rudiments,' but the heavenly bodies, and that the reference is to astrology or the like, is utterly out of place. While the suggestion advanced by Franke on Meyer, that the angels and angel-worship are meant, is too fanciful for serious consideration. Lightfoot has a very clear and able note on the whole passage, defending the view adopted here. **And not after Christ.** Contrast. Here is no robbing philosophy, but the truth of God; no empty delusion, but historical reality; no worldly principles, but divine life, yea, God manifest in the flesh, as the next verse sets forth.

9. For in him dwelleth all the fulness of the Godhead bodily. This declares, in strong and striking language, the true deity of Christ. 'For' here goes back to the turn of expression in the last clause of ver. 8: "Not after Christ," *for*, on the contrary, in him dwelleth, etc. 'In him dwelleth.' The present tense is used here not specially to contrast the present either with the past or with the

future, but simply to denote a prevailing fact, true both of his earthly life and of his present exaltation. And so the vivid use of the present tense simply brings up what must always be true *for us*, a fact ever offered for our perception and acceptance. The ever-present truth is here. 'All the fulness of the Godhead.' For the special appropriateness of using the term 'fulness' because of the Gnostic use of it, see on 1 : 19. The fullness of the Godhead is that which makes Deity complete. The word (θεότης) which would literally be rendered "Godness," if there were such a word, had better be translated Deity rather than Divinity, or, perhaps, even Godhead. Now according to this statement, all that which goes to make up the completeness of God dwells bodily in Christ! Wonderful language! As to the important qualifying word 'bodily,' we may say that it refers to the manifestation of God in Christ, formerly in his earthly body and now in his glorified body. Henceforth (since the incarnation) and forever, the completeness of Deity in bodily manifestation dwells in Christ. Our conception of the Christ while he lived on earth and now when glorified in heaven is that of a bodily fulfillment of God.[1]

With this thought of Christ's fullness of Deity in his mind, Paul goes on to speak of the believer's fullness of Christ. (Ver. 10.) This suggests the spiritual union of believers with Christ under the figure of circumcision (ver. 11); and this naturally leads on to the new rite, which symbolizes the real spiritual entrance of the believer into the main facts in Christ's career, his death and resurrection (ver. 12).

10. And ye are complete in him—ye are filled (Revised Version, "made full"), ye are in a state of completeness in him. Not as he is, the fullness of Deity; but your being filled with all good, with all the excellence of which you are capable, is in and from him. See Eph. 3 : 19. Bengel acutely remarks: "*Ipse plenus,*

[1] Lightfoot well says: "St. Paul's language is carefully guarded: he does not say ἐν σώματι ('in a body'), for the Godhead cannot be confined to any limits of space; nor σωματοειδῶς ('in the form of a body') for

this might suggest the unreality of Christ's human body; but σωματικῶς ('bodily'), 'in bodily wise,' 'with a bodily manifestation.'"

11 In whom also ye are circumcised with the circumcision made without hands, in putting off the body of the sins of the flesh by the circumcision of Christ:

12 Buried with him in baptism, wherein also ye are risen with *him* through the faith of the operation of God, who hath raised him from the dead.

11 head of all principality and power: In whom ye were also circumcised with a circumcision not made with hands, in the putting off of the body

12 of the flesh, in the circumcision of Christ; having been buried with him in baptism, wherein ye were also raised with him through faith in the working

---

nos repleti," he is *full, we are filled.* **Which is the head of all principality and power.** This phrase is not quite clear. It may be either, 1, in general, Christ is superior to all rule or authority; or, 2, especially that he is superior to all orders and ranks of the heavenly beings usually described in these terms. See 1 : 16. The latter is more likely from analogy; and it comes to the same thing, since if he is superior to these he must be over all *inferior* beings, and so his universal supremacy is declared.

11. In whom also ye are circumcised, etc. The rendering of the Revised Version is here decidedly preferable, as better expressing the nice shades of meaning in the original: "In whom ye were also circumcised with a circumcision not made with hands." As the rite of circumcision represented the removal of bodily impurity and the devotion of the circumcised person to God, as one of his peculiar people, so the spiritual union with Christ, here spoken of and represented by the term 'circumcision,' is described as the **putting off the body of the sins of the flesh**—that is, of all carnal incitement to sin. The circumcision spoken of is a spiritual matter **made without hands.** Compare Rom. 2 : 28, 29. Omit 'of the sins' with the best editors on the authority of the most reliable manuscripts. It was a later explanatory addition.[1] 'Body of the flesh' is the body under control of the flesh as suggestive of sin, and being in opposition to God. **By** (*in*) **the circumcision of Christ**—that is, in the renewing of the spiritual life in and by him. Lightfoot says: "The previous verses have dealt with the theological tenets of the false teachers. The apostle now turns to their practical errors: 'You do not need the circumcision of the flesh, for you have received the circumcision of the heart. The distinguishing features of this higher circumcision are threefold: 1. It is not external, but inward; not made with hands, but wrought by the Spirit. 2. It divests

not of a part only of the flesh, but of the whole body of carnal affections. 3. It is the circumcision, not of Moses nor of the patriarchs, but of Christ.' Thus it is distinguished as regards, first, its character; secondly, its extent; thirdly, its author." Is this new circumcision to be identified with the act of baptism? The mention of baptism in the next verse has caused the question to be raised. But there are three reasons why this identification cannot be admitted: 1. The mention of baptism in the next verse is clearly not in the way of *apposition* to circumcision, but only as the mention, in a figurative way, of a rite of the Older Dispensation *suggests* the symbolic rite of the New. There is no word or turn of expression to indicate that baptism was to "take the place of circumcision." 2. In so far as baptism is a humanly-administered (though divinely ordained) rite, it is as much "made by hands" as ever circumcision was. But the circumcision here spoken of is of the heart, and refers to the renewing of the nature which is only outwardly represented in the act of baptism as a burial and resurrection. 3. There is no trace elsewhere in the Scriptures of any identification of circumcision and baptism, or substitution of one for the other. It is hardly too much to say that no one would ever have thought of such an interpretation of this 'circumcision' if the prevalence of infant baptism had not made it desirable for its defenders to seek some Scriptural justification for their practice.

12. Buried with him in baptism. The Revised Version is again decidedly preferable. "Having been buried with him in baptism"— as a symbolic portraiture of that inward change represented as 'putting off the body of the flesh,' and spoken of as a 'circumcision made without hands.' The act of baptism, in which the believer is put under the water, is a symbolic burial to the sins of the past. See Rom. 6 : 3, 4. "For all who in the rite of

---

[1] Westcott and Hort, Tischendorf, Meyer-Franke omit τῶν ἁμαρτιῶν (' of the sins '), following א A B C, etc. It was, no doubt, an explanatory gloss.

13 And you, being dead in your sins and the uncircumcision of your flesh, hath he quickened together
with him, having forgiven you all trespasses;

13 of God, who raised him from the dead. And you,
being dead through your trespasses and the uncircumcision of your flesh, you, *I say*, did he quicken
together with him, having forgiven us all our tres-

baptism are plunged under the water, thereby
declare that they put faith in the expiatory
death of Christ for the pardon of their past
sins; therefore Paul likens baptism to a burial
by which the former sinfulness is buried—that
is, utterly taken away." (Thayer's "Grimm's
Lexicon," p. 605, s. v. συνθάπτω). Lightfoot
(a Bishop of the Church of England) says:
"Baptism is the grave of the old man, and
the birth of the new. As he sinks beneath the
baptismal waters the believer buries there all
his corrupt affections and past sins; as he
emerges, thence he rises regenerate, quickened
to new hopes and a new life." If the learned
bishop meant this to be taken symbolically,
it may be accepted; but if literally, that as an
actual fact this momentous change is effected
by the act of baptism itself, it is of course
much too strong a statement, plainly contrary
to the spirit of New Testament teaching and
to the true meaning of this passage itself.
Wherein also ye are risen with him.
Further symbolism of baptism, a resurrection
to new life. **Through the faith of the operation** (*working,* or *energy*) **of God, who
hath raised him from the dead.** See Rom.
10 : 9. The resurrection of Christ was a glorious exhibition of the mighty energy of God,
and is a central point in the Christian faith.
Now it is faith, dependence on this divine
power, by which this energy becomes effective
"to the saving of the soul." But this reception by faith of the power of God into the life
of the believer is beautifully symbolized in its
effects by the burial and resurrection set forth
in baptism. Compare the more complete expression of the thought in the parallel passage
in Rom. 6 : 1-4.

The mention of Christ's being raised from
the dead by the power of God brings Paul
now to mention (ver. 13) the death in sin from
which the believer is raised by divine power
and forgiveness; this forgiveness is complete,
being evidenced in the entire removal (ver. 14)
of all that makes us obnoxious to the divine

wrath and punishment, a removal by the cross,
in which, though an instrument of shame and
torture, Christ's high triumph (ver. 15) is
achieved.

13. **And you** (emphatic), **being dead in
your sins** (or, *through your trespasses*). 'In'
or 'through'—equivalent here to "by means
of" ; your trespasses were the means of your
spiritual death. 'Trespasses' is the proper
translation. It is the same word that occurs
in the last part of the verse. If Paul could
use it twice in the same sentence, there would
seem no good reason why King James' Revisers should not have done so; but with their
usual fondness for variety, at the expense of
accuracy, they have here rendered it 'sins,'
which is a different word in the Greek. The
word properly translated 'sin' (ἁμαρτία) comes
from a root meaning "to miss," "to go wide
of the mark"; while this word (παράπτωμα)
comes from a word meaning "to fall," "to
fall aside," or "away from the side of." So
both in etymology and usage there is a distinct
shade of difference in the meaning, and they
should not be confounded. Being spiritually
dead by the falls you have made away from
God's law, is the thought. Compare Eph. 2 :
1, seq. **And the uncircumcision of your
flesh**—that is, by your carnal state of aliena-
tion from God; uncircumcision denoting the
natural, ungodly, or rather godless condition
of separation from God. Most probably, it
does not here refer to literal uncircumcision as
the evidence of their being heathen Gentiles
(though possibly suggested by that), but the
figurative use of the term is here continued
for the 'circumcision' of ver. 12. **You, hath
he quickened**—or, *did he quicken.* 'You' is
here repeated, according to the correct text,[1]
not specially for emphasis, but for clearness.
(See Buttmann's Grammar, p. 142.) *Did he
make alive* would be now a more exact rendering, though "quicken" was sufficiently so
in older English usage. **Together with him**
—denoting the close spiritual union with

[1] The best authorities, for sufficient reasons, omit ἐν
('in') before παραπτώμασιν ('trespasses'), and insert a
second ὑμᾶς ("you") after συνεζωοποίησεν ('quick-

ened'). Both readings adopted by the Revisers. So
also ἡμῖν ('us') after χαρισάμενος ('having forgiven')
is undoubtedly the correct text.

14 Blotting out the handwriting of ordinances that was against us, which was contrary to us, and took it out of the way, nailing it to his cross;

14 passes; having blotted out ¹ the bond written in ordinances that was against us, which was contrary to us: and he hath taken it out of the way, nailing it

1 Or, the bond that was against us by its ordinances.

Christ, by virtue of which true spiritual life is given to the believer. "It has been questioned whether the life here spoken of should be understood in a spiritual sense of the regeneration of the moral being, or in a literal sense of the future life of immortality regarded as conferred on the Christian potentially now, though only to be realized hereafter. But is not such an issue altogether superfluous? Is there any reason to think that St. Paul would have separated these two ideas of life? To him the future glorified life is only the continuation of the present moral and spiritual life. The two are the same in essence, however the accidents may differ. Moral and spiritual regeneration is salvation, is life." (Lightfoot, against Meyer.)

An important question of grammar arises here: What is the subject of the verb 'quicken'? God or Christ? It is necessary to understand Christ as the subject of the sentence later on, beginning at the words 'and took out of the way.' The question is whether that construction applies here also, so that we are to regard Christ as the understood subject to 'quicken,' 'having forgiven,' 'having blotted out.' Ellicott takes this position for the sake of uniformity throughout the sentence. But Meyer and Lightfoot more wisely take the ground that we must understand God as the subject in the three cases just mentioned. For these acts are usually ascribed to God, and it is not unnatural or unusual for Paul to glide from one subject to the other in such a connection. See Eph. 2 : 4, 5. No distinct change is made, but the seemingly unconscious passing from one subject to the other is itself most interesting and forcible.

Having forgiven you all trespasses. The correct text (see foot note, page 32) has "us" rather than 'you.' The apostle easily includes himself in the divine forgiveness, though it turns the grammatical construction a little. This divine forgiveness is manifested along with regeneration: 'He quickened . . . having forgiven all your trespasses.'

14. Blotting out—description of the method of the divine forgiveness. Compare Isa. 44 : 22. **The handwriting of ordinances**—

better as in Revised Version, *the bond written in ordinances.* The word (χειρογραφον) means "something written by hand," and so, as we say, "a note of hand" or "bond." See Thayer's "Grimm's Lexicon," p. 668. Not the law of the Decalogue, written by the hand of God, as some have strangely supposed. But it is our obligation to keep the law of God just as if we had given our note of hand; and this is because of its binding nature in general, and because of the consent of reason and conscience thereto. The law promulgated obligates the morally responsible hearer, just as much as a voluntarily assumed debt. For similar modes of expression, though in each case with a different meaning, see Gal. 5 : 3 ; Rom. 8 : 12. On the complete sense here the margin of the Revised Version is best: "the bond that was against us by its ordinances." The quality of this bond, the nature of the obligation involved, is expressed by the term 'ordinances,' or "statutes," or "decrees." These 'ordinances' are those of God given in the law, and the obligation to keep them is 'against us' because it exacts of us more than we can perform. Thus the thought is that we stood indebted by the ordinances of the law; but this debt God forgave; he has canceled the bond. Compare Eph. 2 : 15. It is the standard doctrine of Paul here figuratively set forth, but carefully elaborated in Romans and Galatians. We are delivered from the bondage and penalty of sin by God's grace in Christ. **Which was contrary to us**—besides being 'against us by its ordinances' it is positively hostile, seeking, as it were, our destruction. Compare Rom. 7 : 9-13. **And took (or better,** as in Revised Version, "and he hath taken") **it out of the way**—that is, removed it utterly and forever in its hostile and destructive character. It is the perfect tense in the Greek, expressing the idea that the object remains taken out of the way. It seems better at this point to regard the subject of the verbs in the sentence as changed from "God" to "Christ." This seems more natural and in accord with Paul's usual language. Meyer, however, prefers to consider "God" as the subject throughout, for the sake of grammatical uniformity.

c

15 *And* having spoiled principalities and powers, he made a shew of them openly, triumphing over them in it.

15 to the cross; [1] having despoiled the principalities and the powers, he made a shew of them openly, triumphing over them in it.

[1] Or, *having put off from himself the principalities, etc.*

Nailing it to his cross. The canceled bond is nailed to Christ's cross. Beautiful figure. The Saviour was nailed to the cross and with him our condemnation under the law. It was crucified and knows no resurrection.

> "My soul looks back to see
> The burdens thou didst bear,
> When hanging on the accursed tree
> And hopes *her guilt* was there."

15. This is a very difficult verse. I consider the translation of the Common Version, which also is preferred by the American Revisers, as better than either the text or margin of the Revised Version. **And having spoiled** —that is, despoiled, literally *stripped*, robbed of their power to injure. **Principalities and powers**—here, as the objects of Christ's 'spoiling' and 'triumph,' the *evil* spirits. On this sense, see Eph. 6 : 12, where our "wrestling," spiritual conflict, is against these. **He made a shew of them openly** (or, *boldly*)—that is, he made them before heaven and hell a public spectacle of defeated evil. **In it**—in the cross, which was the token of his lowest humiliation. That in which demons must have rejoiced in short-sighted triumph as *his* overthrow, was really their own. The meaning, then, appears to be this: Christ not only nailed to his cross the canceled bond of our forfeited obligations under the law; but, in that same instrument of shame and yet of glory, he publicly triumphed over those living and active agents of evil who have mysterious power to lead us into temptation and sin; they have such power to corrupt and condemn in some sense because of the law which they lead us to violate; but by nailing the canceled bond of the law to the cross he has despoiled them of one of their best means of injury. This is certainly an intelligible view of the matter, and agreeable to the context. The difficulty in the way—and it is a serious difficulty—lies in the unusual meaning which must be put upon the word translated in the Common Version 'spoiled,' in the Revised Version "put off from himself." The translation of the Revised Version is undoubtedly literal (ἀπεκδυσάμενος). The word really does mean just that, and is, more-

over, found in its correct signification in this very Epistle. (3:9.) "Having put off from yourselves the old man." But what meaning can we get from the words if a literal translation be adhered to? The Revised Version reads: "Having put off from himself the principalities and the powers, he made a shew, etc." What can this mean? Can it be that the terms 'principalities and powers' here do not refer to living beings, but to the high authority with which Christ was clothed and which he laid aside to die on the cross, so that we have here a similar passage to Phil. 2:7? This will not do: (1) because the words are invariably elsewhere used of spiritual beings, good or bad; and (2) because there could be no propriety in saying that Christ 'triumphed over' the exaltation which he laid aside in dying on the cross. No; we must hold fast the notion that 'principalities and powers' have here their usual meaning of spiritual beings. But are they good or bad? The good angels cannot be meant, because Christ did not 'triumph over' them in the cross. We are shut up then to the view that these terms here refer to those evil forces and intelligences which are spoken of again in Eph. 6 : 12, which have power over the minds of men to lead them to sin and destruction. Now, then, the question is: In what sense could Christ be said to 'put off from himself' the evil angels? Lightfoot tries hard to justify this interpretation, as follows: "Christ took upon himself our human nature with all its temptations. (Heb. 4 : 15.) The powers of evil gathered about him. Again and again they assailed him; but each fresh assault ended in a new defeat. . . . . The final act in the conflict began with the agony of Gethsemane; it ended with the cross of Calvary. The victory was complete. The enemy of man was defeated. The powers of evil, which had clung like a Nessus robe about his humanity, were torn off and cast aside forever. And the victory of mankind is involved in the victory of Christ. In his cross we too are divested of the poisonous clinging garments of temptation, sin and death." But notwithstanding this special pleading it is very strange that 'principalities and powers' should

16 Let no man therefore judge you in meat, or in drink, or in respect of a holyday, or of the new moon, or of the sabbath *days*:

16   Let no man therefore judge you in meat, or in drink, or in respect of a feast day or a new moon or

be conceived of as a *garment clinging to Christ's humanity*. It is a hopeless incongruity; and the reference Lightfoot makes to the "filthy garments" of Joshua and the presence at the same time of "Satan," in Zech. 3 : 1–4, sounds more like one of the Fathers than a great scholar of these scientific days. One other resort is left for those who will hold to the literal meaning of the word ('having disrobed,' 'having put off' from himself'); and that is to understand after it, "his body," and render as the margin of the Revised Version: "Having put off from himself *his body*, he made a shew of the principalities and powers." This would undoubtedly give a plain and scriptural meaning to the expression, but we have no grammatical right to insert an object after a verb simply to make the meaning clear, unless that object is either involved in the meaning of the verb itself, or can be plainly gathered from the context as having been in the writer's mind. Neither of these conditions is found here. The only object naturally suggested by the verb would be a garment not a body, and if so unusual an idea as putting off a body were intended, the object would have to be expressed. Again the thought of Christ's body is too remotely suggested by the nailing of the bond to the cross to make it necessary or even likely that it should be inserted here as an object to a verb (participle) which has already one plain grammatical object. Besides all this, it must be plain from the structure of the sentence that Paul intended 'principalities and powers' to be the object of 'having put off.' We are compelled, therefore, to seek for some other meaning for this term than the common one of disrobing, putting off from oneself. If the participle were in the active voice there would be no difficulty, for the verb means to 'strip off,' 'to divest entirely of'; but in the middle voice of the Greek verb it means to 'strip off' from oneself,' 'to divest oneself entirely of.' But besides this purely reflexive use of the middle voice there is another known to gram-

marians; and that is that it describes the action, not as directly performed on oneself, but as being done with reference to oneself, or for one's own advantage. Here we must take refuge in this secondary use of the middle voice in the Greek; that is that Christ 'stripped' the 'principalities and powers,' not himself; but that he did so with a view to his own glory in the triumph of the cross. Thus we come to the meaning which has already been explained. It is not without difficulty, but it has less objection than any of the others proposed. Meyer upholds this view.

The apostle makes now more definite allusion to the forms of error which then threatened the Colossian Christians. In ver. 16, 17, we have, accordingly, a warning against ceremonialism.

16. Let no man therefore judge you. 'Therefore' points back to the triumphant expiatory work of Christ. The force of the exhortation is: Do not, by subjecting yourselves to ceremonial requirements which are done away in Christ, make yourselves liable to the fanatical judgment and censure of ascetical persons. **In meat or in drink**—or, "eating and drinking."[1] This refers to ceremonial, and, doubtless, extremely rigid requirements as to clean and unclean articles of food and drink. **Or in respect of a holyday**, etc. The Revised Version is more accurate: "Or in respect of a feast day, or a new moon, or a sabbath day." The claims of these observances were, no doubt, greatly exaggerated, and, possibly, made tests of fellowship. There is danger of such things all the time. The warning is not idle. The use of the term 'sabbath' in this connection may have some bearing on the much-mooted question of Sabbath observance in our own days. The question is too broad for full discussion here, but two things may be remarked: 1. The literal Jewish sabbath, the seventh day, may be meant as being no longer the day for Christians to observe, the Lord's Day being substituted and sufficient. 2. Or that the peculiar

---

[1] Whether to read ἐν βρώσει ἢ ἐν πόσει, 'in meat *or* in drink,' or ἐν βρώσει καὶ ἐν πόσει, 'in meat *and* in drink." The point is unimportant and the difference slight. The common reading has the strongest docu-

mentary evidence, and is retained by Tischendorf. The other reading is adopted, though not decisively, by Lightfoot, Westcott and Hort, after B and a few others.

17 Which are a shadow of things to come; but the body *is* of Christ.

18 Let no man beguile you of your reward in a voluntary humility and worshipping of angels, intruding into those things which he hath not seen, vainly puffed up by his fleshly mind.

17 a sabbath day; which are a shadow of the things 18 to come; but the body is Christ's. Let no man rob you of your prize [1] by a voluntary humility and worshipping of the angels, [2]dwelling in the things which he hath [3]seen, vainly puffed up by his fleshly mind,

1 Or, *of his own mere will, by humility, etc* ......2 Or, *taking his stand upon* ......3 Many authorities, some ancient, insert not.

Jewish exaggerated mode of keeping the sabbath should not be insisted on. We are not to suppose that the observance of the sabbath, which is as old as the Creation and enjoined in the Decalogue, is to be entirely done away, as being only a shadow. (Ver. 17.) **Which are a shadow of things to come.** These ceremonies had their valuable use; but they are the shadow only of the eternal verities revealed in Christ. Compare Heb. 9 : 11 and 10 : 1. Question arises as to the significance of 'things to come.' The present tense, 'which *are* a shadow,' is, as Ellicott observes, not to be unduly pressed, because it is the "general present" stating things according to their nature and relations, rather than with special reference to time. It would be confusing to refer the 'things to come' to the future state, the glories of heaven, as these are not now under consideration. It is more natural to regard the expression as describing the revelation of the Christ, which the Jews were accustomed to speak of as "the age to come." (Heb. 2:5.) The remark is made from the standpoint of the Old Testament, as Olshausen correctly observes. **But the body is of Christ** —or, *Christ's.* This is not the appositional genitive, equivalent to saying, the body *is* Christ; but it means that the substance of all these things is in Christ, their true reality and significance is in him ; they are only shadows of realities which exist in them. So is it unwise to pay more regard to these ceremonial matters than to the solid truths taught by Christ and his apostles.

In the next two verses (18, 19) we have a distinct and pointed warning against the false teachers at Colosse.

18. Let no man beguile you. The Revised Version here is far better: "Let no man rob you of your prize." The word is unusual (καταβραβεύειν), derived from the prize (βραβείον) given in contests. The literal meaning is to award unfavorable judgment as umpire, whereby a contestant is deprived of the prize ; and so, *to deprive* (or rob) *of a prize.* The 'prize' here alluded to is that mentioned

in Phil. 3 : 14 as the object of Paul's own earnest efforts, " the prize of the high calling of God in Christ Jesus." He pleads: "Take care lest these teachers of false things lead you astray and cause you to miss that prize." Compare ver. 8. The expression need not be considered contradictory to the doctrine of the Perseverance of Saints, which is not here in question: as a doctrine, but, like all other such warnings, is to be taken as one of the means to perseverance. Paul goes on now to set forth the manner of the robbery by describing the character of the robber. **In a voluntary humility.** This is certainly a wrong translation, and it is wholly surprising that the Revised Version retains it. Nor is even the marginal rendering of that Version correct. It has not even given us a good alternative. The truth is that the phrase is exceedingly difficult, and the Revisers have simply evaded it by retaining the incorrect rendering of the Common Version in their text, and giving one of a number of commentators' guesses in the margin. It is not likely that any translation will be satisfactory. Hort supposes that there is here a "primitive corruption of text" which has been perpetuated in all our existing authorities. But the authorities we now have are decisive as to the reading, and it is dangerous to attempt conjectural emendation. It is rather a cheap way of avoiding a difficulty. The commentators, as was surely to have been expected, differ very much among themselves in dealing with the knot—verily, a *crux interpretum.* To bring the difficulty clearly before the English reader, let us take a literal translation : " Let no man rob you of your prize, willing in humility and worship of the angels." The trouble evidently lies in the interpretation of the participle "willing" (θέλων). Literally rendered as above, it gives no apparent sense. Various renderings (mostly guesses) have been proposed, such as that of the Common Version and of that of the margin of the Revised Version ; but only two seem to have any just claim to probability: 1. " Let no man rob you willing—wishing, purposing—(to do so) in humility," etc. This is the view of Meyer (not Franke) and of Ellicott. It is grammatically allowable, and gives a passable sense. The objections to it are (1) that the participle 'willing' would really thus be superfluous, and (2) it does not harmonize so well with the context; for the following words, 'in humility,' etc., will then have to be taken either as the means (Meyer) or the sphere (Ellicott) of the robbery, instead of describing the character of the robber, as the rest of the passage does. The other, and preferable proposal, is to give a different and unusual translation to the participle, and read : 2. "Let no one rob you of your prize *delighting* in humility," etc. This affords excellent sense and accords well with the context. The apostle is describing the sort of person who would defraud them of their heavenly prize, and in so doing incidentally shows the method of his procedure; he is one who takes pleasure in humility and angel worship, who launches out into visions that he has seen, who is vainly puffed up in his carnal mind, and who does not hold on to Christ, from whom all really true and profitable spiritual teaching comes. The only question is, Have we a right to translate the participle "delighting" or "taking pleasure"? It must be admitted that the word does not have this meaning in classical Greek, nor does it occur in this sense elsewhere in the New Testament. But it is true that in the Septuagint exactly this phrase (θέλων ἐν), 'willing in,' occurs quite frequently, as a translation of the Hebrew expression "to delight, or take pleasure in" a person or thing. Thayer's "Grimm's Lexicon" gives the examples, which are numerous, sufficient to establish the point, and should be decisive.[1] Buttmann, in his "New Testament Grammar," opposes this view, but

with conspicuous ill-success for so great a scholar. Ellicott dismisses it too sweepingly ; Lightfoot defends it with force. There is no valid objection to it on any ground, except its unusualness; but with the Septuagint usage so well made out, and with the somewhat similar usage of the word in Matt. 9 : 13; 27 : 43, and Heb. 10 : 5 (all quotations from the Septuagint), we need not fear to allow that Paul uses the term here in its unclassical and unusual Septuagint sense. If this be allowed, the meaning becomes plain : "Taking pleasure in humility"—that is, in a profession of exceeding humility, said from the standpoint of the man himself, descriptively. **And worshipping of angels**—that is, this person feels too humble to worship God ; he must stop short of the Infinite One and worship intermediate beings! 'Humility'—real lowliness of mind, is, of course, a good thing, an eminent Christian virtue. But this was (and ever is) a sad perversion. We must worship God humbly, but we are not too humble to worship him at all. As Lightfoot well says : "There was an officious parade of humility in selecting these lower beings as intercessors, rather than appealing directly to the throne of grace."

The person warned against is further described as **intruding into those things which he hath not seen**. The Revised Version reads: "dwelling in the things that he hath seen"; in the margin, "taking his stand upon the things that he hath seen." The 'not' in the Common Version must be omitted before 'seen,'[2] and 'intruding' is not a correct translation of the Greek word ἐμβατεύων. The Revisers' text, "dwelling in," is nearly correct, but inadequate and somewhat misleading; their margin, "taking his stand upon," is more literal and somewhat explanatory, but not yet quite satisfactory. The word

[1] Ps. 111 (112) : 1 ; 146 (147) : 10 ; 1 Sam. 18 : 22 ; 2 Sam. 15 : 26 ; 1 Kings 10 : 9 ; 1 Chron. 28 : 4 ; 2 Chron. 9 : 8.

[2] There is a very important and difficult variation here. The Received Text has ἃ μὴ ἑώρακεν ('things which he hath not seen '), on authority of אᶜ C Dᵇᶜ K L P many cursives (F G have οὐκ), f g Vulgate, Gothic, Syriac, Armenian, Origen (in some passages), Chrysostom, Euthalius, Theodoret, and others. Westcott and Hort, Tischendorf, Lightfoot, Meyer-Franke have ἃ ἑώρακεν (or ἑώρακεν) (' things which he hath seen,' omitting the negative), on the decisive authority of א* A B D* 17. 28. 67** d e m Coptic, Arabic, Ethiopic, Origen (two passages), Tertullian, Lucifer. Jerome and Augustine

mention that the manuscripts differed in their day. From the early and strong documentary evidence we can only conclude that the negative was a later insertion to smooth over a difficulty. With the negative the sense is easy; without it, very difficult. But is it necessary to resort, with Lightfoot and Hort, to "conjectural emendation"? What advantage is to be gained by rejecting, on strong documentary grounds, a well-supported manuscript emendation, and resorting to one that has no manuscript authority (and but little plausibility, for that matter) in its favor? For the interpretation, see the comment.

19 And not holding the Head, from which all the body by joints and bands having nourishment minis- tered, and knit together, increaseth with the increase of God.

20 Wherefore if ye be dead with Christ from the rudiments of the world, why, as though living in the world, are ye subject to ordinances,

19 and not holding fast the Head, from whom all the body, being supplied and knit together through the joints and bands, increaseth with the increase of God.

20 If ye died with Christ from the [1] rudiments of the world, why, as though living in the world, do ye

---

1 Or, *elements*.

---

literally means "going into," "embarking on," and is used in classical Greek and in the Septuagint in quite a variety of senses noted by Thayer's "Grimm's Lexicon" under the word. The meaning here appears to be, "launching forth upon things that he has seen"; that is, going into detailed statements about wonderful things that he has seen, harping upon his visions, telling more than he or anybody else can prove. The caustic description proceeds: **Vainly puffed up by his fleshly mind.** *This* is a good translation, and the meaning is clear at a glance. The mind is the moving power, but it is here represented as controlled by 'the flesh'; that is, the lower nature, the sinful propensities. Thus it is inflated with a sense of its acquisitions, but 'vainly'; that is, to no good purpose. "Their profession of humility was a cloak for excessive pride." (Lightfoot.) The final touch is put to the portrait now:

19. And not holding the Head—that is, of course, Christ. These false teachers in their wild vagaries departed from the "simplicity that is in Christ," they taught not "as the truth is in Jesus." This is the decisive test. Whatever teaching does not accord with the truth of Christ ought to be avoided. **From which** (or, *whom*)—that is, Christ. The change of the relative pronoun is significant. **All the body by joints**, etc. The Revised Version is rather clearer: "From whom all the body being supplied and knit together through the joints and bands increaseth," etc. The 'body' is the "church," the body of believers, and so the effects here described apply severally to each believer. 'Being supplied' with spiritual nourishment, 'and knit together,' compacted, strengthened in spiritual life and power; 'through the joints and bands,' whatever connects with the Head, as faith, love, obedience, on our part, and presence, grace, and care, on Christ's. It would be incongru-

ous to suppose with some that the 'joints and bands' refer to individual members of the body. Nor yet is it well to press the figure too far, as that the 'joints' are faith, the 'bands' love, and such like. Ellicott well says: "The passage does not seem so much to involve special metaphors as to state forcibly and cumulatively a general truth." **The increase of God** is the growth and enlargement of spiritual character, which is ministered of God's grace by the Spirit, and which God therefore expects and requires. "By the twofold means of contact and attachment nutriment has been diffused and structural unity has been attained, but these are not the ultimate result; they are only intermediate processes; the end is *growth*." (Lightfoot.) See the similar passage in Eph. 4 : 15, 16.

20-23. Asceticism.—In the remainder of the chapter the warning is especially directed against *asceticism*, which was also a prominent feature of the false teachings to which the Colossians were exposed.

20. Wherefore if ye be dead with Christ. Omit 'wherefore,'[1] and read as in the Revised Version: "If ye died with Christ from the rudiments of the world." The 'if' here does not express doubt as to the fact of their having died, but has its argumentative use: if it be a fact, then, etc. The dying with Christ is viewed as past because of Christ's death as a past event, and because of their own experimental dying with him being a fact which occurred on their spiritual union with Christ by faith. When they accepted Christ as Saviour and Lord, they entered into that real and vital union with him which makes his death their death, both as a penalty for sin and as a complete renunciation of the old life of sin. See 2 Cor. 5 : 14, 15; Gal. 2 : 19, 20; 6 : 14. The argument here is from this renunciation. "If ye have renounced this old life of conformity to the world, why try in a measure to

---

1 Westcott and Hort, Tischendorf, Lightfoot, and Meyer-Franke all omit οὖν ('therefore') after εἰ ("if"), on decisive authority. It was a later addition.

21 (Touch not ; taste not; handle not ;
22 Which all are to perish with the using ;) after the
commandments and doctrines of men?

21 subject yourselves to ordinances, Handle not, nor
22 taste, nor touch (all which things are to perish with
the using), after the precepts and doctrines of men?

live it over again?" See also 3 : 1. For the symbolic representation of this great change in baptism, see 2 : 13. The note on ver. 8 explains what is meant by 'rudiments of the world.' **Why, as though living in the world**—that is, as if you were still moved and controlled by worldly principles. **Are ye subject to ordinances?**—that is, to the opinions and decrees of men. These 'ordinances' of men have no real authority in themselves, and are only 'rudiments of the world' at best —why allow them to be imposed on you?

21. Touch not, etc. The Revision more accurately translates: "Handle not, nor touch, nor taste"—a sort of climax of prohibition. The words are emphatic, but there is no need to suppose that each refers to a different class of objects from the other, as the first to unclean vessels, the second to dead bodies, the third to unclean food, and the like. It is more natural to take them all as referring to such articles of food and drink as the ascetic rules forbade. It was probably an established formula of asceticism, and is quoted as an example of their teachings—the kind of 'ordinance' which the Colossians were not to allow to be imposed upon them. It is a grievous misinterpretation of the meaning, and misapplication of the words to use them as being themselves a Scriptural command, and as applying to strong drink. There are passages which teach the right attitude of the Christian toward the sin of drunkenness, but this is not one of them. The rigid asceticism which finds expression in this formula is precisely what the apostle condemns.

22. Which all are to perish with the using. The grammatical construction here is difficult and uncertain. The difficulty is occasioned, however, by the parenthetic clauses alone. If they be omitted the construction is easy and the meaning plain: "Why do ye subject yourselves to ordinances after the precepts and doctrines of men?" The two inserted clauses, 'Handle not,' etc., and 'Which all are to perish,' etc., are the cause of trouble; and of these chiefly the second. The clause 'Handle not,' etc., is evidently a quotation of a sample of the 'ordinances' to be avoided. The gist of the diffi-

culty therefore lies in the relation of the relative clause, 'Which all are to perish with the using,' to the other. The question is twofold: (1) The proper connection of the two clauses, and (2) the proper meaning of the second clause. But, of course, these are mutually dependent, and cannot well be discussed separately. Three interpretations may be considered: (1) The Revised Version puts only the second of the two clauses in a parenthesis, thus taking it as a passing remark of the apostle. He observes parenthetically that all those things which the quoted ascetic rule requires should not even be touched, are in fact made to be destroyed in the use of them. Their use is to be used up; they are for destruction by using up; and it is therefore idle to make of these perishable things a great test principle in morals. This view is held by the majority of the best expositors. Meyer, Lightfoot, and Ellicott all agree on it. There is no doubt that it seems upon the whole the most satisfactory, but the others deserve notice. (2) The Common Version puts both clauses in the same parenthesis, and thus makes it all a quotation of an ascetic maxim. The second clause is also the language of asceticism, and gives a reason for the prohibition contained in the first. So in this view the matter is to be thus understood: The ascetic says: Handle not, nor taste, nor even touch these things, all which are to perish with use. Leave them all alone; they are unsafe to meddle with; they are mere material things, unworthy of an instructed man's notice; they are even corrupt in tendency, and to touch them is defiling. This interpretation is harsh and improbable, though possible. (3) Another view would put the two clauses in the same parenthesis, still making both the language of the ascetic, but would give a different interpretation to the phrase 'perish with the using.' The Greek literally is, 'Which all are for destruction by the use.' Now, the word rendered 'use' (ἀπόχρησις) is a compound word with the idea of "using up" or "over using," and so may mean *excessive* use, or *abuse*. It is in fact found in this sense. And the 'perishing' referred to may be that of the *person using*, as well as of the *things used*. Hence it is gram-

23 Which things have indeed a shew of wisdom in will-worship, and humility, and neglecting of the body; not in any honour to the satisfying of the flesh.

23 Which things have indeed a shew of wisdom in will-worship, and humility, and severity to the body; but are not of any [1] value against the indulgence of the flesh.

1 Or, honour.

matically and exegetically possible to render the phrase thus: "Which all make for destruction by abuse"—that is, if a man abuses these things it will tend to his own ruin, and he had better not even touch them. The complete ordinance of the ascetic then would be: "Handle not, etc., all these material things commonly used as food and drink, for by excessive use of them a man is certain to be ruined." Now the principle is sound within due limits, but its exaggeration is nonsense. While it is true that abuse of eating and drinking causes ruin, the inference is not abstain entirely, but use in moderation; the former would be rigid asceticism, the latter Christian common sense. This is a plausible view, but it lacks simplicity. Lightfoot says of it: "It loses the point of the apostle's argument, while it puts upon 'are to perish' a meaning which is at least not natural." It cannot be said that any one of these interpretations is entirely satisfactory, but the first is less objectionable than the other two, and is therefore adopted as the best that can be made of a difficult phrase.

After the commandments and doctrines of men—and not by the authority and example of Christ, for he was himself no ascetic and taught no asceticism. This quotation of Isa. 29 : 13 (Septuagint) and the teaching itself of the passage according to the interpretation adopted above remind us forcibly of our Lord's teaching in Matt. 15 : 1-20 and Mark 7 : 1-23. It is not improbable, as Lightfoot says, "that the apostle had this discourse in his mind."

23. Which things have indeed a shew of wisdom—literally, a word of wisdom, and so an argument which has appearance of wisdom, and so a repute of wisdom. There is nothing so contrary to sound common sense and wholesome Christian doctrine but may find plausible advocacy. The apostle goes on to state wherein consists this 'word of wisdom.' In will-worship—that is, in a self-imposed religious observance, not required by

Christ, but set up by man, and made to appear as clear inference from established principles. And humility—an excellent virtue, often assumed for a purpose. See above on ver. 18. And neglecting of the body.[1] The Revised Version is better, "severity to the body"—that is, unsparing ascetic discipline, fasts, vigils, etc. The three elements of the 'shew of wisdom'—worship, humility, and self-denial —have a very taking power with some people, and have bolstered many a hurtful error, because, in their proper place and degree and kind, they are pillars of the truth. Falsehood always is more dangerous when it can take and use the watchwords of truth. The apostle turns now to deny the true value of such ascetic practices. Not in any honour to the satisfying of the flesh—or, as Revised Version renders: "But are not of any value against the indulgence of the flesh." They break down right where their value is claimed; they do not offer any valid safeguard against carnal indulgence. This seems to be the best interpretation of a confessedly difficult and obscure phrase. We may agree with Hort that "none of the current explanations are satisfactory," that is, wholly satisfactory, but it is rather daring to suppose here again "primitive corruption of text" when there is no trace of such corruption in our existing documents. Would it not be better to suppose that in the current colloquial language of the time, or in the cant of the ascetics, or in the local usage of the Colossians, there lay a peculiar shade of meaning in some of these terms that is not apparent to us? The newspaper dialect of to-day would suggest difficulties of interpretation, even to a student in our own tongue, a hundred years hence; and yet a grave philosophical or religious treatise might find it most effective to use language that by reas n of local or temporary coloring would become rather obscure in later times. Now, there may have been such local or temporary coloring of meaning in the words rendered

[1] Lightfoot, Westcott and Hort, bracket καὶ ('and') before ἀφειδίᾳ ('severity'), on authority of B and some lesser authorities. Tischendorf retains. Better, I think.

"honor" or "value," and "satisfying" or "indulgence," as made the sentence perfectly clear and forcible to the Colossians, while its meaning is obscure to us. Three renderings and interpretations should be considered:

1. That of the Common Version: 'Not in any honour to the satisfying of the flesh.' That is, these ascetic practices have an *apparent* justification in self-made formulas of religious worship and the like; but they have no such justification, or 'shew of wisdom,' in any honor they confer as regards the satisfying of the natural and reasonable demands of the body. That is to say, it confers no honor on a man to neglect these natural demands and despise his own body by subjecting it to useless and absurd ascetic rigors. The fatal objection to this view is that the word 'satisfying' (πλησ-μόνη) does not in correct usage describe the natural, moderate, and proper gratification of the bodily desires, but their excessive and improper gratification. The interpretation therefore is untenable, as contrary to the usage of the word, and, though held by some of the Greek Fathers, is rightly rejected by the best modern expositors.

2. The interpretation of Meyer: Which things have a reputation for wisdom in self-imposed service and humility—not in anything which is really an honor—for the sake of satisfying the flesh. The words 'not in any honor' he regards as somewhat parenthetical, containing a remark in passing. So it means that these 'ordinances and doctrines' of the ascetics have a reputation for wisdom in order thereby to furnish full indulgence to the "natural man." That is, it comes about that while one is having reputation for wisdom in ascetic severities to the *body*, he is really working to satisfy to the full his *carnal nature* in the sense of spiritual pride, power over others, and the like. This interpretation has itself 'a shew of wisdom' in conjunction with such passages as Gal. 6: 12, 13 and Rom. 16: 18, but it is too artificial. It is adopted and defended by Ellicott, but rejected by Lightfoot for excellent reasons: (*a*) that it breaks the connection of the sentence, and so is grammatically objectionable; and (*b*) that it gives a meaning to the words 'satisfying of the flesh' that is forced and unnatural.

3. The interpretation of the Revised Version: "But are not of any value against the indulgence of the flesh." These things may have 'a shew of wisdom,' so far as self-imposed worship and humility and severity are concerned; but they are of no value or worth whatever as a safeguard against any real temptation to bodily indulgence. Ascetic observances do not make a man pure, or shield him against fleshly temptations. This interpretation approves itself as agreeable to the context, grammatically smooth, and not distorting in any way the meaning of the words 'satisfying of the flesh.' It is open, however, to two objections, but these are not as serious as those which lie against the other two views. The difficulties are: (*a*) In translating the Greek word for 'honor' (τιμή) as 'value.' But this meaning, though rare, is not unknown, being found in various writers, as Lightfoot has clearly shown. It may also have this sense in 1 Peter 2 : 7, while adjectives derived from it are commonly used for "valuable," "costly," etc. See Matt. 13 : 46; 26 : 7; John 12 : 3; 2 Peter 1 : 1. (*b*) In translating the Greek preposition meaning 'for' (πρός) by the word "against"; but this also is allowable in usage, as Lightfoot again has proved. Yet these are felt to be objections, and the passage remains difficult, but this is the only interpretation that is at all satisfactory. Lightfoot puts it well in a paraphrase: "All such teaching is worthless. It may bear the semblance of wisdom, but it wants the reality. It may make an officious parade of religious service; it may vaunt its humility; it may treat the body with merciless rigor; but it entirely fails in its chief aim. It is powerless to check indulgence of the flesh."

HOMILETICAL SUGGESTIONS.

Ver. 2: A trilogy of consolation: 1. Mutual love. 2. Intelligent faith. 3. Growing knowledge. The first a condition, the second an acquisition, the third a consummation. **Ver. 6:** The orderly Christian walk, according as we have received by faith the Christ: 1. As Saviour. 2. As Teacher. 3. As Exemplar. 4. As Lord. **Ver. 7:** The true Christian character: 1. Rooted and building up in Christ. 2. Confirmed and steadied by faith. 3. Thankful in spirit. **Ver. 8:** 1. Warning against intellectual captivity. 2. Instrument of such captivity. 3. Character of the instrument. **Ver. 9:** 1. Careful explanation of

CHAPTER III.

IF ye then be risen with Christ, seek those things which are above, where Christ sitteth on the right hand of God.
2 Set your affections on things above, not on things on the earth.
3 For ye are dead, and your life is hid with Christ in God.

1 If then ye were raised together with Christ, seek the things that are above, where Christ is, seated 2 on the right hand of God. Set your minds on the things that are above, not on the things that are 3 upon the earth. For ye died, and your life is hid

the text, 'Godhead,' 'fulness,' 'dwelleth,' 'bodily.' 2. Inferences from the text, (a) the Deity of Christ, (b) divine character, power, and purpose in Christ, (c) superiority of Christ, therefore, to 'philosophy and vain deceit.' **Ver. 10 :** How our fullness of Christ differs from Christ's fullness of God. See John 1 : 16; Eph. 3 : 19. **Ver. 12:** Mode and meaning of baptism. Relation of baptism. 1. To circumcision. 2. To faith. 3. To salvation. **Ver 13, 14:** Two contrasts. 1. Death and life. 2. Debt and forgiveness. **Ver. 14 :** The completeness of the divine pardon; he has canceled the bond. **Ver. 15:** The glorious triumph of Christ over all the evil powers by the cross. **Ver. 16 :** The rights of the individual conscience with regard to ceremonial observances must be respected. A truth that needs repeated enforcement. **Ver. 17:** Shadow and body, forms and principles. Forms have their uses, 'but the body is of Christ.' **Ver. 18, 19 a:** Description of the spiritual robber: 1. Professing humility—the agnostic. 2. Too humble to worship God directly — the worshiper of nature, of humanity, of the saints. 3. Proclaiming a new light—the spiritualist, the devotee of "Christian Science," and others like them. 4. Full of self-conceit—the whole set. 5. Denying Christ—all of them again. **Ver. 19 :** Union with Christ: 1. Nourishment supplied. 2. Strength imparted. 3. Increase made. **Ver. 20 :** Contrasted conditions: 1. Death with Christ. 2. Life in the world. The one implies contradiction to the other. **Ver. 20-22:** Christianity opposed to rigid asceticism. **Ver. 23:** 1. Asceticism has plausibility. 2. But not true value.

Ch. 3 : 1-4. Exhortation to Seek the Things Above.—Passing now, in accordance with his usual custom, from the more distinctly doctrinal to the more distinctly hortatory, the apostle begins this part of the Epistle with an exhortation appropriately deduced

from the glorious doctrines he has been teaching, and appropriately leading to the particular precepts he is now about to enforce. The translation of the Revised Version is preferable.

1. If ye then be risen (or, *were raised*) **with Christ.** The exhortation corresponds to that in 2 : 20. Here, again, the 'if' does not imply doubt, but has its argumentative force. The 'then' goes back to 2 : 20, and both together to the burial and resurrection symbolically set forth in baptism. (2:12.) 'Were raised.' The past indefinite refers to the time of their conversion symbolized in baptism. 'With Christ' signifies in spiritual union with him. Compare Rom. 6 : 4, 5 (Revised Version) and 1 Peter 1 : 3. By the same power which raised him from the dead, and because of his resurrection, were you raised from moral and spiritual death to the new life in him. **Seek those things which are above**—that is, make heavenly things the objects of your aims and efforts. How natural and just the inference: if you *have* a heavenly life-principle, *live* a heavenly life. **Where Christ sitteth**—rather, Where Christ *is*, seated on the right hand of God; that is, since his resurrection. The locality, and the presence of Christ there, characterize the objects of the believer's purposes. The further description, 'seated on the right hand of God,' figuratively expresses the union of Christ with God in the possession of divine power and authority, and is, hence, a further reason for seeking heavenly things. Compare Rev. 3 : 21.

2. Set your affection (not only your 'affection,' but your mind) **on things above.** Repetition for emphasis, change of expression for fullness: Let these heavenly things occupy your thoughts as well as be the objects of your search. **Not on things on the earth.** Emphatic contrast.

3. For ye are dead—literally, *ye died;* not 'ye are dead,' by no means! you are alive

4 When Christ, *who is* our life, shall appear, then shall ye also appear with him in glory.

5 Mortify therefore your members which are upon the earth; fornication, uncleanness, inordinate affection, evil concupiscence, and covetousness, which is idolatry :

4 with Christ in God. When Christ, *who is* [1] our life, shall be manifested, then shall ye also with him be manifested in glory.

5 Put to death therefore your members which are upon the earth; fornication, uncleanness, passion, evil desire, and covetousness, the which is idolatry ;

1 Some ancient authorities read *your.*

now—past tense again, as above, expressing the time of union with Christ by faith. The change of figure from ver. 1, from resurrection with Christ back to death with Christ as preceding resurrection, is expressive. You must have 'died' first, in order to "rise," hence the 'for.' So did you 'die' to sin and the common pursuits of this life, from the 'elements of the world.' Between you as unregenerate and as regenerate, there should, therefore, exist a separation as complete as death. See 2 : 20; 2 Cor. 5 : 14, 15. And **your life** (you still have a life, and a better one) **is hid with Christ in God.** Note the change of tenses: "Ye died" is past indefinite, or aorist; 'your life is (or, *has been*) hidden' is perfect, and so remains unto the present. "The aorist denotes the past act, the perfect the permanent effects." (Lightfoot.) 'Life' is here to be taken in its completed power and reality, not in its beginnings; for these are possessed even here. Jesus said: "Whosoever believeth on me *hath* everlasting life." (John 6 : 47.) But this life in its fullness, in its consummated perfection, is *hid,* as treasure laid up "where neither moth nor rust doth corrupt, and where thieves do not break through nor steal." It is treasured up with Christ, where the sources and strength of its present degree of manifestation lie, 'in God.' Thus, both in the source of its present power and in the fulfillment of its reality, it is 'hid' —not visible to the natural eye, not fully grasped by the faculties of the human intellect.

4. When Christ, who is our life, shall appear. '*Our* life.' The apostle gladly associates himself with those to whom he writes, in the possession of this inestimable treasure.[1] Our life is not only *with* him, but he *is,* in fact, the life itself. Compare John 1 : 4 and 14 : 6.

Christ, as the source and cause and keeper of life for us, *is* really our life. 'Shall appear' —or, "shall be manifested;" that is, at his second coming. **Then shall ye also appear with him**—or, *be manifested;* that is, shown in your true character as his, as instinct with the life which he is. **In glory**—that is, not only splendidly, gloriously, but in the state of 'glory.' See on 1 : 27. It refers to their being made manifest in the consummation of the gospel, and is not to be confined to the glorious beauty of their appearance after the resurrection.

5-11. Exhortations Appropriate to the New Life.—Those who are blessed with such hopes, and animated by such purposes as have been just described, should constantly repress the degrading tendencies of the lower nature "which warreth against the soul."

5. Hence, Mortify therefore your members which are upon the earth. For 'mortify,' unwisely retained by the Revised Version, it is best to read 'put to death,' with the American Committee. Like many other words, 'mortify' has come to have a different and weakened sense in modern usage, and is no longer an adequate rendering of the vigorous original, 'make dead.' Some authorities omit 'your,' reading, simply, "the members." [2] The variation does not in the least affect the meaning. By the expression 'members which are upon the earth' is meant the parts and functions of the body which lead to sin, the seat of sin being figuratively put for the sin itself. These sins now follow as apposition : **Fornication, uncleanness, inordinate affection** (*passion*), **concupiscence** (*evil desire*). These are different names and forms of the same vice, then, and now, and ever terribly prevalent. **And covetousness, which is idolatry.** This sin is spe-

---

1 Doubtful whether we should read ἡ ζωὴ ἡμῶν ('*our* life'), or ἡ ζωὴ ὑμῶν ('*your* life'). ℵ C D * F G P, with other strong authorities, favor ὑμῶν ("your"), and this is adopted by Tischendorf. B Dᵇᵉ K L, and other fewer, but respectable authorities, have ἡμῶν; and this is adopted (not positively) by Lightfoot, Westcott and

Hort, Meyer-Franke. It is rather preferable on internal grounds, but it is impossible to decide positively.
² Westcott and Hort, Tischendorf, Lightfoot, Meyer-Franke all omit ὑμῶν ('your') after μέλη ('members'), with the more weighty, though less numerous, authorities.

6 For which things' sake the wrath of God cometh on the children of disobedience:
7 In the which ye also walked sometime, when ye lived in them.
8 But now ye also put off all these; anger, wrath, malice, blasphemy, filthy communication out of your mouth.

6 for which things' sake cometh the wrath of God
7 [1] upon the sons of disobedience; [2] in the which ye also walked aforetime, when ye lived in these
8 things. But now put ye also away all these; anger, wrath, malice, railing, shameful speaking out of

1 Some ancient authorities omit *upon the sons of disobedience.*   See Eph. v. 6......2 Or, *amongst whom.*

---

cially emphasized here: 1. By being mentioned along with the defiling vices. 2. By being singled out from the rest by the article (which the Revised Version vainly attempts to bring out in an awkward way). 3. By being characterized as 'idolatry.' The word, too (πλεονεξία), is very suggestive in its etymology. It denotes the character of one who desires "*to have more*"—that is, more than he has (*discontent*), more than others have (*envy*), more than he ought to have (*injustice*). It is 'idolatry' because it is worship of mammon. (Matt. 6 : 24.)

6. **For which things' sake the wrath of God cometh**—the punitive wrath of God in his holy abhorrence of sin. The present tense ('cometh') may be taken to mean 'is ever coming' as a matter of actual experience and observation; or simply as 'will certainly come' because it is a fixed law of the divine government. The latter conception is probably the correct one here. **Upon the children of disobedience.** Some authorities omit this clause as an interpolation from Eph. 5 : 6; but the evidence is not, to me, convincing.[1] The meaning is: "Upon those who are by these sins disobedient to God." The mode of expression is frequently employed in the Bible. One who is specially marked by the *character* of a thing (whether person, object, or quality) is called a *child* of that thing, it being natural for a child to resemble its parent.

7. **In the which.** Read, 'in which'; there is no use in retaining this awkwardness of the Common Version, and, as there is no article in the Greek, the Revised Version, by retaining it here discredits its own use of the phrase in ver. 5, as already noticed. If the rendering

'in which' (neuter) be preferred, the reference is of course to the sins previously mentioned; and this it will have to be if the words 'upon the children of disobedience' be omitted. But if they be retained the rendering "among whom" may be adopted and the reference will be to the sinners rather than to the sins. This is grammatically equally as good as the other, and a little preferable as it relieves the saying from being a truism. I prefer, therefore, to render: "Among whom ye also formerly walked (as being yourselves such as they) when ye lived in these things"—that is, in these evil affections and deeds. Your *conduct* was that of children of disobedience when your *life* was marred by these evil things. The correct text is "these," not simply "them" as in Common Version.[2] But there is some uncertainty both about the reading, and as to the reference of "these," since it also may be either neuter or masculine. But upon the whole the rendering adopted above seems to me the most likely.

8. **But now**—emphatic, as contrasted with your former life. **Ye also put away all these.** The 'ye also' is emphatic too. Do even you, who were formerly such as described, now put away these things. Then follows another list of evil things to be put away: **Anger, wrath**—the former, rather settled indignation; the latter, boiling passion. But in such lists as these we are not so much to look for nice shades of meaning in the words themselves as to mark the emphasis brought out by the accumulation of so many terms of kindred meaning. **Malice** is wicked grudging, evil wishes for others. **Blasphemy** is here injurious, slanderous speech against each other, not against God in this connection.

---

[1] The words ἐπὶ τοὺς υἱοὺς κ. τ. λ. ('upon the sons of disobedience') are omitted by Westcott and Hort, Tischendorf, Lightfoot, Meyer-Franke on the authority of B; some versions and Fathers, as an evident interpolation from Eph. 3 : 6. But there is no inherent impossibility, or very great improbability, that the apostle should use the phrase in both places. And it

may well be questioned whether the consideration of the same language in two places should *always* weigh against valuable and strong evidence, as here.
[2] Westcott and Hort, Tischendorf, Lightfoot, Meyer-Franke all read ἐν τούτοις ('in these things') instead of ἐν αὐτοῖς ('in them') on decisive authority.

9 Lie not one to another, seeing that ye have put off the old man with his deeds;
10 And have put on the new *man*, which is renewed in knowledge after the image of him that created him:
11 Where there is neither Greek nor Jew, circumcision nor uncircumcision, Barbarian, Scythian, bond nor free: but Christ is all, and in all.

9 your mouth: lie not one to another; seeing that ye
10 have put off the old man with his doings, and have put on the new man, who is being renewed unto knowledge after the image of him that created
11 him: where there cannot be Greek and Jew, circumcision and uncircumcision, barbarian, Scythian, bondman, freeman: but Christ is all, and in all.

Filthy communication out of your mouth—obscene, abusive language.

9. Lie not one to another. This completes the thought; lying goes with the rest. **Seeing that ye have put off**—literally and simply, 'having put off'; but with a suggestion of an argumentative force involved in the participle, and hence not incorrectly given in the versions. The word has here its proper force of "putting off" from oneself as a garment." Compare 2 : 14. **The old man**—your former self. See ver. 7. **With his deeds**—his characteristic actions. The old *ways* must be put away along with the old experiences.

10. And have put on—literally and simply again "and having put on," but with the same argumentative force going on. **The new man**—that is, a new life in and with Christ and by virtue of repentance and faith. The better way of acting toward each other is, not only to have laid aside old ways, but to have put on new ones also. The character of this 'new man' is now to be described. **Which is renewed in knowledge.** The Revised Version is better: "Which is being renewed unto knowledge"—that is, is undergoing renewal toward and up to the point of reaching right knowledge of things divine. It is a new life, and its newness becomes apparent in growing knowledge of the things of God. The phrase 'renewed,' made new *again* (ἀνά) seems to point to the original purity of man before the Fall, and this is further borne out by the allusion to his creation in what follows. **After the image of him that created him.** This growth in spiritual knowledge is to result in the restoration of that likeness of God in which man was created, and which was marred by his sin.

11. Where—that is, in a community composed of these new men who are being renewed in God's likeness. **There is neither Greek nor Jew.** Scholars are not unanimous as to the exact meaning of the curious little word (ἕνι) rendered 'there is;' in the

Revised Version "there cannot be." It is either a contraction of a well-known word (ἔνεστι), signifying "it is possible"; or an enlargement of the preposition 'in' (ἐν), with the idea of the verb "to be" added. If the latter, it is properly rendered as the simple substantive verb, as in the Common Version. But if the former view be preferred, it is, with the negative, to be given as in the Revised Version. This is most probably the correct view, and the meaning is that in such a state of things the ordinary human distinctions of rank, race, religion, and the like can no longer prevail, for all are *new* men. Translate then as follows: *Where there can no longer be Greek and Jew, circumcision and uncircumcision, barbarian, Scythian, bondman, freeman.* Compare Gal. 3 : 28. The antipathies of Greek and Jew, of Judaism and heathenism, shall have no place; barbarians shall be subdued, and Scythians, the worst of barbarians, softened, by the gospel; even the galling distinction of slave and free shall be done away.[1] Lightfoot has a long and interesting note on the passage which is worthy of study. But it does not seem necessary in a brief commentary like this to go into extended discussion, since the meaning is clear without it. This glorious state of renewal and elevation finds its acme in the statement: **But Christ is all, and in all.** Instead of current distinctions that divide and embitter men, Christ is everything; all differences merge in him; all good things are summed up in him; all things worth having and worth being are to be sought and found in him; instead of the passions and jealousies that flourish in the unrenewed heart, Christ shall be in every man the motive of his life, the principle and the controlling power of his new existence. The presence and the power of Christ, in his own love, shall overrule all distinctions and obliterate all jealousies. Others take the phrase to mean : "Christ *is* all things and *in* all things," taking in both cases 'all' as

[1] The best authorities omit καί ('and') after δοῦλος ("bondman").

12 Put on therefore, as the elect of God, holy and beloved, bowels of mercies, kindness, humbleness of mind, meekness, longsuffering;

13 Forbearing one another, and forgiving one another, if any man have a quarrel against any: even as Christ forgave you, so also do ye.

14 And above all these things put on charity, which is the bond of perfectness.

15 And let the peace of God rule in your hearts, to the which also ye are called in one body; and be ye thankful.

12 Put on therefore, as God's elect, holy and beloved, a heart of compassion, kindness, humility, meekness, 13 longsuffering; forbearing one another, and forgiving each other, if any man have a complaint against any; even as [1] the Lord forgave you, so also do ye: 14 and above all these things put on love, which is the 15 bond of perfectness. And let the peace of Christ [2] rule in your hearts, to the which also ye were called

---

1 Many ancient authorities read *Christ*..... 2 Gr. *arbitrate.*

---

neuter. That is to say, Christ in this renewed state of mankind is the sum of all things, and the pervasive principle of all things. The meaning is about the same in either case and either is grammatically admissible, but it seems rather better to take the second 'all' as masculine and referring to those who are renewed. (Eph. 3 : 17 : Col. 1 : 27.)

12-17. VARIOUS PRACTICAL EXHORTA-TIONS.

12. Put on therefore, as the elect of God, holy and beloved. Paul urges now as a consequence ('therefore') of their having put off the old man with his deeds, and having put on the new man, a temper and conduct suitable to their dignity and character as the *chosen*, the *holy*, and the *beloved* of God. The 'holy and beloved' are not vocative, but further explanatory adjectives, along with 'elect.' The 'therefore' may refer, as Lightfoot understands it, to the last preceding words. 'Christ is all, and in all'; but owing to the similarity in expression regarding 'put off' and 'put on,' it seems better with Meyer to refer it to ver. 9. 'Holy'—not in the sense of absolute sinless perfection, but as belonging exclusively to God as his chosen, and therefore separated from common uses and ends. **Bowels of mercies**—rather, as Revised Version, *a heart of compassion.*[1] The viscera were regarded by the ancients as the seat of the emotions, especially those of this character. **Kindness**—or, gentleness. **Humbleness of mind**—that is, 'humility,' now used in the best and usual sense, and not as in 2 :

18, 23. **Meekness**—not a heathen virtue. **Longsuffering**—patient endurance of evil. **13. Forbearing** and **forgiving** go beautifully together. **If any man have a quarrel against any**—rather, "complaint," as Revised Version. It may be even a *just* complaint. **Even as Christ** (or, 'the Lord')[2] **forgave you, so also do ye.** The highest measure of forgiveness. But it is better to take these words as beginning a new sentence: "Even as the Lord forgave you, so also (do) you (forgive each other)." This is more natural than to consider the participial structure as going on.

14. And above all these things put on charity—that is, "love." In addition to all these virtues, put on the including element of them all; over and above, as taking them all in, and hence called **the bond of perfectness.**[3] There is some little difficulty in getting at the exact meaning of this beautiful phrase. It may be either (1) the bond which by uniting all virtues tends to perfection, puts the finishing touch upon character; or (2) simply the Hebraistic adjective relation, the bond which is characterized by perfectness, the bond which is perfect as a bond. Other views also are held by various expositors, but Lightfoot well expresses what seems the best sense thus: "The power which unites and holds together all those graces and virtues which together make up perfection."

15. And let the peace of God[4] (or, more correctly, *of Christ*) **rule in your hearts.** The 'peace of Christ' is the peace which he

---

1 Best authorities read οἰκτιρμοῦ ("of mercy" sing.) instead of οἰκτιρμῶν ("mercies").

2 Hard to decide whether to read ὁ χριστὸς ἐχαρίσατο ('Christ forgave') with Tischendorf, after ℵ° C D b and ° E K L P, almost all cursives, many versions, and Fathers; or ὁ κύριος ("the Lord forgave") with Westcott and Hort (text), Lightfoot, Meyer-Franke, after A B D* F G 213; d e f g m Augustine, Pelagius. ℵ* has θεὸς

("God"), which is clearly a correction. The reading of Westcott and Hort more probably correct.

3 Ὁ ('which,' neuter) is undoubtedly the correct reading, though harsh grammar.

4 Ἡ εἰρήνη τοῦ χριστοῦ ("the peace of Christ"), instead of τοῦ θεοῦ ('of God') is the reading of Westcott and Hort, Lightfoot, Tischendorf, Meyer-Franke, after decisive authority: ℵ A B C D, etc.

16 Let the word of Christ dwell in you richly in all wisdom; teaching and admonishing one another in psalms and hymns and spiritual songs, singing with grace in your hearts to the Lord.

16 in one body; and be ye thankful. Let the word of [1] Christ dwell in you [2] richly; in all wisdom teaching and admonishing [3] one another; with psalms and hymns and spiritual songs singing with grace

1 Some ancient authorities read *the Lord:* others, *God*......2 Or, *richly in all wisdom*......3 Or, *yourselves.*

bestows (John 14:27), and which must produce a peaceable spirit in him who receives and keeps it. For the translation 'rule,' the margin of the Revised Version substitutes "arbitrate." The word is derived from the deciding of an umpire (βραβεύς) at the games, and comes to mean "arrange," "direct," "control," and so "rule." (Meyer, Ellicott.) But no doubt the primary meaning is to "render a decision as umpire," "to arbitrate." If this original meaning be adopted, the exhortation amplified would be this: "Be at peace among yourselves, in accordance with the peace-loving disposition imparted to you in the gift of the peace of Christ; let this peaceable spirit decide all differences among you, moving your own hearts." Or, as Lightfoot puts it: "Wherever there is a conflict of motives or impulses or reasons, the peace of Christ must step in and decide which is to prevail." But these interpretations are a little cumbersome, and the simpler meaning 'rule' is probably to be preferred, being sustained by good usage. **To the which** (leave out 'the') **also ye were called in one body**—that is, "you were called of God to be at peace with one another, even as one body, animated by one life principle." **And be ye thankful.** Not an afterthought, but thanksgiving is a real result of peace, and is to be returned to God for peace.

16. **Let the word of Christ dwell in you richly.** The 'word of Christ' is the gospel, the doctrine, the teaching of Christ, both information and precept. 'Dwell in you richly' —a striking phrase; dwell in your being as a home (ἐνοικείτω), with all its riches of spiritual help, abundantly influencing your life. We have in the remaining words of this verse a great difficulty in properly arranging the clauses. When it is remembered that the ancients wrote without punctuation, and without spaces between the words, it will be seen how impossible it is to tell in every case exactly what arrangement of clauses was in the

writer's own mind. We must depend on the sense, but, as several different arrangements may give equally good sense, sometimes it is largely a matter of taste and feeling with each expositor what special order he shall adopt. It is interesting to notice the different ways in which this sentence may be read by changing the punctuation: (1) 'Let the word of Christ dwell in you richly in all wisdom; teaching and admonishing,' etc. (2) 'Let the word of Christ dwell in you richly'; 'in all wisdom teaching,' etc. (3) 'Teaching and admonishing one another in psalms,' etc.; 'singing with grace in your hearts to God.' (4) 'In all wisdom teaching and admonishing one another'; in psalms, etc., with grace singing in your hearts to God. (5) 'Teaching and admonishing one another in psalms, etc., in grace'; 'singing in your hearts to God.' Now, upon a careful comparison of these various ways of combining the words of the sentence, it is evident that any of them gives sense, and may be grammatically adopted. Naturally the expositors adopt and combine them very variously. My own preference is to hold on to the punctuation of our Common Version, and to render as follows: *Let the word of Christ dwell in you richly in all wisdom; teaching and admonishing one another in psalms, hymns, spiritual songs; with gratitude singing in your hearts unto God.* The exposition is accordingly based on this view of the relation of the clauses. 'Let the word of Christ dwell in you richly in all wisdom'— that is, let the gospel principles and precepts fully direct and control your life, so that its power may be manifest in a conduct marked by eminent wisdom; your wise demeanor will betray the rich sources of spiritual force dwelling within you. 'Teaching and admonishing one another in psalms, hymns,[1] spiritual songs.' They were to use these spiritual exercises as a means of mutual instruction and warning. Observe the construction of 'teaching and admonishing'; it is what is called the "abso-

[1] The best authorities omit the conjunction καὶ (' and ') before both 'hymns' 'and spiritual songs,' making vivid style.

17 And whatsoever ye do in word or deed, *do* all in
the name of the Lord Jesus, giving thanks to God and
the Father by him.
18 Wives, submit yourselves unto your own husbands,
as it is fit in the Lord.

17 in your hearts unto God. And whatsoever ye do,
in word or in deed, *do* all in the name of the Lord
Jesus, giving thanks to God the Father through
him.
18 Wives, be in subjection to your husbands, as is

lute" construction, no subject being expressed.
"You" is of course implied. It gives a
slightly imperative sense to the words, and is
peculiarly emphatic: ' Let the word of Christ
dwell in you richly—you, under such influence, teaching,' etc. The grammatical smoothness is interrupted for emphasis. The different
shades of meaning in the terms ' psalms,
hymns, spiritual songs,' are interesting, as
showing the various kinds of songs used in
worship by the Christians of the apostolic age.
It seems most likely that the ' psalms' were
those of the Old Testament translated, and
possibly otherwise modified to suit the needs
of public worship; the ' hymns' were songs
of praise to God, not only Old Testament
psalms of this character, but no doubt others
also; the ' spiritual songs' or ' odes' were
other songs, not specially included in the preceding; perhaps songs of devotion, experimental, even historical, but they must be
' spiritual,' that is, in general, devout, moved
by the Holy Spirit and elevating the spirit of
the worshiper. Some suppose we have a speci-
men of such an ' ode' in the words of 1 Tim.
3 : 16, which appear to be a quotation and are
somewhat metrical. Singing with grace¹ in
your hearts unto God. Probably "gratitude" is here a better rendering than ' grace.'
Compare Heb. 12 : 28. It is not perfectly
clear what meaning is to be preferred. (1)
Some say "gracefulness," that is, acceptable-
ness, that which gives pleasure to the object.
This does not accord very well with the sense
of this passage, though the word occurs with
that meaning, most probably, in 4 : 6 of this
Epistle, and has other support in New Testament usage. See Luke 4 : 22; Eph. 4 : 29.
(2) Others say "grace" in the sense of the
divinely bestowed favor, the usual New Testament use of the word. The occurrence of the
article here, as if *the* divine grace, so often
mentioned in Paul's writings as the highest of
our privileges, were intended, gives force to
this interpretation; and the meaning will be

that worship is to be rendered in the enjoy-
ment of divine grace, viewed (as is sometimes
the case) as an active quality of our own, because received and embraced by us. (3) But
as this is rather labored it is simpler to take
' grace' here as meaning "gratitude," notwithstanding the article, which is emphatic—
the gratitude which is appropriate, which we
ought to have, etc. The word frequently has
this sense in the New Testament, as well as in
classical Greek, and seems here more appropriate to the context. Some hold that the expression ' in your hearts' points to a *silent*
singing of the grateful heart to God as distinguished from the mutual edification of the
openly sung ' psalms, hymns, and spiritual
songs.' But this seems a forced and unnatural
sense to put on the words. While we teach
each other in the ' psalms and hymns and spiritual songs,' let the singing of them be at the
same time a grateful exercise of the heart
toward God.
17. And whatsoever ye do in word or
deed—a very general exhortation, all-inclu-
sive. In the name of the Lord Jesus—
as the element or sphere of the doing. Nothing unworthy of Christ is to be done, nothing
unfit to be said or done in the closest association with him, but everything in such a way
that the holy presence and character of Christ
will not be offended. Giving thanks to God
and the Father through him. Much better to omit the ' and,' as it is wanting in the
Greek. Christ is Mediator of God's grace to
us and of our acceptable worship to God.
3 : 18-4 : 1. Domestic Duties.—Compare
the similar passages in Eph. 5 : 22-6 : 9, where
the discussion is more extended; 1 Tim. 6 : 1,
2; Titus 2 : 1-10; 1 Peter 2 : 18-3 : 7. It is
natural that, after the general exhortation of
ver. 12 and following, Paul should more especially emphasize Christian duty in the important relations of the household.
18. Wives, submit yourselves unto your
own husbands (or, better, as in the Revision,

¹ Westcott and Hort, Tischendorf, Lightfoot, Meyer-
Franke all have ταῖς καρδίαις, ' hearts,' instead of singular ' heart,' upon decisive authority : א A B C D, etc.

So also τῷ θεῷ (" to God "), instead of τῷ κυρίῳ (" to the
Lord ").

19 Husbands, love *your* wives, and be not bitter against them.
20 Children, obey *your* parents in all things: for this is well pleasing unto the Lord.
21 Fathers, provoke not your children *to anger*, lest they be discouraged.
22 Servants, obey in all things *your* masters according to the flesh; not with eyeservice, as menpleasers; but in singleness of heart, fearing God:

19 fitting in the Lord. Husbands, love your wives
20 and be not bitter against them. Children, obey your parents in all things, for this is well-pleasing
21 in the Lord. Fathers, provoke not your children,
22 that they be not discouraged. [1]Servants, obey in all things them that are your [2]masters according to the flesh; not with eyeservice, as menpleasers, but

1 Gr. *bondservants*. ......7 Gr. *lords*.

be in subjection to your husbands). The best authorities omit 'own' before 'husbands.' The *limits* of a wife's becoming subjection to her husband are not laid down, but the *thing itself* is clearly taught here, as elsewhere, by Paul. Did he foresee that abuse would be made of the blessings brought to woman by the gospel? Were such abuses even then beginning to appear? And is that why he addresses himself *first* to wives, although giving to the husband the first place in the home? **As is fitting in the Lord.** Christianity teaches, and is in so far committed to what is *fitting* in this respect. The unfit is unchristian. Literally, the expression is, "as *was* fitting," and the use of the imperfect tense has been variously explained. It is probably best to say, after Meyer, that it expresses what is a general truth, but is only *imperfectly realized* as a fact in the present.

19. Husbands, love your wives—the appropriate and beautiful counterpart of a wife's due submission. **Be not bitter against them**—that is, hasty, quarrelsome. Ever wise and needed admonition!

20. Children, obey your parents in all things. This supposes that the parents are worthy of obedience, and their commands are not contrary to God's commands. So there are conceivable cases when a child would be justifiable in disobedience, but the general rule is explicit and urgent, and Christian parents should carefully see to its enforcement. **For this is well pleasing unto** (or, *in*[1]) **the Lord**—in that sphere of duties and proprieties of which the Lord is the centre and sum and life. Christianity sanctifies this relation also.

21. Fathers, provoke not your children to anger. Do not tantalize them with petty exactions and wanton tyranny. **Lest they be discouraged.** How expressive! A child

is easily disheartened by cruelty, or even a lack of sympathy. A valuable hint.

22. Servants, obey in all things your masters according to the flesh. Slavery being then an existing institution, the apostle gives precepts suitable to its proper regulation. There are Christian duties growing out of the relations on both sides. It is noteworthy that more is said here to servants than to the others. This is probably due in part to the fact that many of this unhappy class were found among the early converts to Christianity, and they were often depraved and wicked; and partly also to the case of Onesimus which was then fresh in the apostle's mind. This man had wronged his master, Philemon, and fled to Rome, where he had met with Paul and was converted to Christ, and was then caused by the apostle to return and submit himself to his master. See the Epistle to Philemon, which was probably sent along with this letter. Of course, as in the case of children, there are supposable limits to the obedience even of a slave, and they are reminded that the relation itself is 'according to the flesh.' **Not with eyeservice**—service that must be watched to see that it is done at all, or properly done. Some authorities give the word in the plural, "eyeservices," and this would be expressive of the various single acts of such service. **As menpleasers**—solely desirous of pleasing men without any reference to the right or wrong of the matters themselves. **But in singleness of heart**—without the double dealing involved in mere 'eyeservice' for pleasing. **Fearing God** (or, *the Lord*[2])—looking ultimately beyond the earthly relation to the Lord, in fear of doing what is wrong in his sight. Crimes, though often caused by injustice, are not excused by hatred.

1 Westcott and Hort, Tischendorf, Lightfoot have *ἐν κυρίῳ* ('in the Lord'), instead of simply *τῷ κυρίῳ* ('to the Lord') on decisive authority.
2 Question whether to read *ὀφθαλμοδουλίαις* ('eye-

services,' plural), or *ία* (singular). Preference is rather for plural form. Westcott and Hort, Tischendorf, Lightfoot have *τὸν κύριον* ('the Lord'), instead of *τὸν θεόν* ('God'), on decisive authority.

D

23 And whatsoever ye do, do *it* heartily, as to the Lord, and not unto men;
24 Knowing that of the Lord ye shall receive the reward of the inheritance: for ye serve the Lord Christ.
25 But he that doeth wrong shall receive for the wrong which he hath done: and there is no respect of persons.

23 in singleness of heart, fearing the Lord: whatsoever ye do, work [1] heartily, as unto the Lord, and not
24 unto men; knowing that from the Lord ye shall receive the recompense of the inheritance: ye serve
25 the Lord Christ. For he that doeth wrong shall [2] receive again for the wrong that he hath done: and there is no respect of persons.

1 Gr. *from the soul*........2 Gr. *receive again the wrong.*

---

23. And whatsover ye do, etc. The same thought put in different words. All the service, even of a slave, should be dutifully and faithfully done, from the heart, not by external compulsion, with a view to what the Lord thinks of it, and not only men.

24. Knowing that of the Lord ye shall receive the reward of the inheritance. Genitive of apposition, same as saying "the reward which is the inheritance." Rich reward, indeed, the inheritance of God's children! Slaves by earthly law, but freemen in Christ, and so "children of God" and "joint heirs with Christ." Sometimes, but very rarely, were slaves made heirs of their masters; seldom enough and often enough to give point to this expression. Such language accordingly must have had great comfort for the unfortunate class to whom it was addressed. Gibbon adduces as one of the causes of the rapid spread of Christianity in early times the hopes it held out, and the blessings it brought, to the slaves. And why not, pray? Does not that religion *deserve* to spread that brings blessing and offers hope to the lowest as well as the highest of mankind? The systems of philosophy do not so much. **For**[1] **ye serve the Lord Christ.** This is your real bondage, you belong to Christ by the purchase of his blood, and the right of almighty sovereignty. Or it may be imperative: "Serve the Lord Christ." Let your service range higher than your earthly masters, and be directed to Christ. It is hard to decide with any positiveness of conviction, but the indicative is rather preferable.

25. But—rather, *for*.[2] 'For,' as a consequence of your service to Christ, not as a consequence directly of his Lordship, though it *may* be that. Yet the thought rather is that true service to Christ (see Matt. 25: 31-46) is the criterion of merit. In the rewards and punishments of the Great Day no mistakes will be made. **For he that doeth wrong.** The question arises whether the wrong doer is the master, or the slave, or either. Lightfoot takes it that both may be intended; the wrong doer, whether master or slave, shall receive his due punishment. This is very likely in itself, and is ably justified by Lightfoot. Meyer, on the other hand, is very decidedly of the opinion that the unjust master is meant, by way of encouraging the slave. The slave must be faithful and good in his own place, for the Lord will see that the unjust master is punished. Others take it that Paul means here to warn the eye-serving, man-pleasing slave that if he defrauds his master he will surely be punished for his sin; his condition will not justify crime. Either way gives good sense. But I see no good reason against including both senses, as Lightfoot does. **Shall receive for the wrong which he hath done**—literally, "*shall receive the wrong*"; that is, in its appropriate penalty the wrong itself will come back upon the wrong doer. How often demonstrated even in the judgments of time! **And there is no respect of persons.** God will not be more lenient in judging a slave because he is a slave than in judging a master because he is a master. God will not show partiality because of these earthly distinctions. The sentiment applies whichever view of the preceding phrase be taken.

Ch. 4 : 1. This is one of several places where the division of chapters in our Bibles is exceedingly unfortunate. The intelligent reader is, of course, aware that the chapter and verse divisions in our copies of the Scripture are not the work of the inspired writers themselves, but were introduced gradually for convenience of reference and comparison, and were received and fixed as they stand at pres-

---

[1] א A B C D * E 17: 47. 71.; Vulgate, Coptic, Arabic; Euthalius, Pelagius, followed by best editors omit γάρ ('for') before τῷ κυρίῳ.

[2] The best authorities all have γάρ ('for'), instead of δέ ('but').

CHAPTER IV.

MASTERS, give unto *your* servants that which is just and equal; knowing that ye also have a Master in heaven.

1 1 Masters, render unto your ²servants that which is just and ³ equal ; knowing that ye also have a Master in heaven.

1 Gr. *lords* ......2 Gr. *bondservants* ......3 Gr. *equality.*

ent—the chapters just before and the verses probably after, the invention of printing. They have nothing but the authority of convenience and custom to commend them. It is surprising that any one who could read should have thought it proper to make a division here.

Masters. How beautifully does the apostle turn to these now, with the duties appropriate to *their* station ! **Give unto your servants that which is just.** 'Give,' or, better, *render. Giving* is not in question ; it is the rendering of justice. Even a slave has his rights before God and man, and he must be treated *justly.* This was new doctrine in that day. **And equal**—literally, as margin of the Revised Version, "and equality." In the matter of justice and right, put them upon the same footing as any one else; for justice and right must be done for their own sake—there must be no respect of persons. Meyer prefers this view, interpreting the 'equality' to refer to moral and spiritual matters, and not to any subversion of the relations of slaves, or the overthrow of the social order. Lightfoot and Ellicott, however, prefer to render the word "equity," "do unto your servants that which is just, and equity "; for the word (ἰσότης) has that meaning sometimes, and the context would seem to favor such an interpretation here. But it seems to me it would be rather tautological, as well as awkward, to say "that which is just, and equity" ; so I prefer 'equality,' understanding it, as Meyer does, of moral and spiritual matters, which are here under consideration. The preceding advice to the slaves, as well as his treatment of Onesimus, shows that Paul did not mean 'equality' in any socialistic or revolutionary sense. **Knowing that ye also have a Master in heaven.** If only all earthly masters were like *him,* how different all things might be ! So they who are masters must remember their own Heavenly Master, who will do equal and exact justice to all, certainly including those who abused the earthly relation by injustice and oppression.

HOMILETICAL SUGGESTIONS.

Ver. 1: 1. Condition—if truly a believer. 2. Duty—seeking heavenly things. 3. Encouragement—Christ seated in power. **Ver. 2 :** 1. Thoughtful consideration of heavenly, rather than earthly, things. 2. There is great need of it. 3. Great reasons for it. 4. Great blessing in it. **Ver. 3 :** 1. Complete separation, as by death, from worldly things. 2. New life in Christ stored up; not yet in full view. **Ver. 4 :** 1. Christ the life. 2. Christ manifested. 3. ' Ye also.' **Ver. 5 :** The only right thing to do with some things is to *kill* them.—Covetousness: 1. Its company. 2. Its character. **Ver. 6 :** 1. God has wrath. 2. His wrath cometh, now and hereafter. 3. The cause of his wrath. 4. The objects of his wrath. **Ver. 8 :** Emphasis of a change—putting off anger, and all the other evil things. Always in order thus to emphasize one's conversion. **Ver. 9 :** Truthfulness between man and man a *necessary* consequence of the new life. A much-needed lesson to-day in society, in trade, in politics. **Ver. 10 :** The new man is renewed man. The renewed man is intellectual man. The intellectual man, so renewed, is man in the image of his Creator. **Ver. 11 :** Human distinctions: 1. How they arose. 2. Why they continued to exist. 3. In what sense they are to be obliterated—not all of them, in fact, for that could not be; but in their abuses and evils. 4. How they are to be thus done away—not by anarchy and bloodshed on one side, nor by pride and oppression on the other ; but by the prevalence of Christian principles, by the indwelling and overruling power of the Christ. The supremacy of Christ:—1. The sum of all *things.* 2. The power for good in all *men.* **Ver. 12, 13 :** 1. The Christian's standing 'with God — elect, holy, beloved. 2. The Christian's corresponding attitude toward men—compassion, kindness, etc. **Ver. 14 :** The perfection of love as the bond uniting Christians. **Ver. 15 :** The ruling power of peace! **Ver. 16 *a* :** Complete application of Christ's teaching is greater wisdom in action. **Ver. 16 *b* :** The right kind

2 Continue in prayer, and watch in the same with thanksgiving;
3 Withal praying also for us, that God would open unto us a door of utterance, to speak the mystery of Christ, for which I am also in bonds:
4 That I may make it manifest, as I ought to speak.
5 Walk in wisdom toward them that are without, redeeming the time.
6 Let your speech *be* always with grace, seasoned with salt, that ye may know how ye ought to answer every man.

2 Continue stedfastly in prayer, watching therein
3 with thanksgiving; withal praying for us also, that God may open unto us a door for the word, to speak the mystery of Christ for which I am also in
4 bonds; that I may make it manifest, as I ought to
5 speak. Walk in wisdom toward them that are
6 without, 1 redeeming the time. Let your speech be always with grace, seasoned with salt, that ye may know how ye ought to answer each one.

1 Gr. *buying up the opportunity.*

of church music: 1 That which promotes mutual edification. 2. That which has a distinctly religious character. 3. That which is acceptable worship to God. **Ver. 17:** Broadest of all precepts, as widely reaching as possible, capable of universal application, covering all "doubtful cases," including all wrong things not specially singled out for Scriptural condemnation! Do only those things that are: 1. In harmony with the pure name of Christ. 2. That we can praise God in doing. **Ver. 18-4:1:** Series of discourses on the cardinal domestic duties in the light of the gospel; or *one* discourse dealing with all four at once would be useful. **Ver. 23:** May have a useful application to others besides slaves. **Ver. 24, 25:** The final test is not *station*, but *action*. **Ch. 4:1:** Though primarily written for masters who owned their servants, it has also appropriate application to employers, and needs to be heeded by all who purchase, as well as compel, the services of others.

Ch. 4: 1 properly belongs at the end of the last chapter. See above.

2-6. Various Exhortations.

2. Continue in prayer. The Revised Version inserts "stedfastly," not because of any word found in other texts, but only because the notion of perseverance is involved in the word rendered 'continue' (*προσκαρτερεῖτε*). **And watch in the same**—more literally, the Revised Version, " watching therein." Compare Mark 14:38. " Keep your hearts and minds awake while praying." (Lightfoot.) **With thanksgiving.** This must ever be an element of true prayer, and is often so urged by the apostle. **3. 4. Withal praying also for us.** He asks for these prayers now on behalf of himself and his co-laborers in the gospel. **That God would open unto us a door of ut-**

terance—literally, "a door of the word." Genitive of the object, and therefore rightly given in the Revised Version, "a door for the word;" that is, enlarged opportunity for preaching the gospel. Compare 1 Cor. 16:9. **To speak the mystery of Christ**—that is, the revelation of God in Christ, the gospel. See note on 1:26. Ellicott remarks that the genitive is here that of the *subject*, it is "the mystery of which Christ is the sum and substance." This is probably correct, though others put slightly differing constructions upon it, but the same general sense. **For which** (that is, the 'mystery,' or the whole notion of speaking the mystery) **I am also in bonds.** A special personal reference. Paul was then a prisoner at Rome (not Cesarea; see the "Introduction") for the sake of the gospel, having been sent thither by Festus as related in the closing chapters of the Acts. **That I may make it manifest**—that is, the 'mystery.' It must not remain a 'mystery' in the narrower sense. **As I ought to speak.** For the force of this 'ought,' compare the following passages: Jer. 20:9; Matt. 10:27; Acts 9:15, and 22:21; 1 Cor. 9:16; 2 Cor. 4:13.

5. Walk in wisdom toward them that are without—that is, act with prudence and tact toward those who are not believers. **Redeeming the time.** Compare Eph. 5:16. This *may* mean rescuing the time from idle uses and employing it for spiritual good to others; but the decidedly preferable meaning is that given in the margin of the Revised Version. "Buying up the opportunity"—that is, seizing the fitting occasion for doing good as a merchant " buys up" commodities at the right time for profit. With an eye to the best effect, make use of opportunities for the salvation of others, especially in the use of speech, as the following verse shows. **Let your speech be always with grace**—not

7 All my state shall Tychicus declare unto you, *who is* a beloved brother, and a faithful minister and fellow servant in the Lord:

8 Whom I have sent unto you for the same purpose, that he might know your estate, and comfort your hearts;

9 With Onesimus, a faithful and beloved brother, who is *one* of you. They shall make known unto you all things which *are done* here.

10 Aristarchus my fellow prisoner saluteth you, and Marcus, sister's son to Barnabas, (touching whom ye received commandments: if he come unto you, receive him;)

7 All my affairs shall Tychicus make known unto you, the beloved brother and faithful minister and fellow-servant in the Lord: whom I have sent unto you for this very purpose, that ye may know our estate and that he may comfort your hearts; together with Onesimus, the faithful and beloved brother, who is one of you. They shall make known unto you all things that *are done* here.

10 Aristarchus my fellow-prisoner saluteth you, and Mark, the cousin of Barnabas (touching whom ye received commandments: if he come unto you, receive

here the divine grace, but rather "attractiveness," giving pleasure to those who hear. (See note on 3 : 16.) But this, of course, not at the expense of truth or faithfulness. **Seasoned with salt**—having force and character; not insipid, but pointed. There may be reference also to the preservative and purifying power of salt. Let your speech be wholesome, not corruptive. But this is not so natural as the other. It is scarcely possible that there is reference to *wit;* though 'salt' is often used in that sense in the classics. **That ye may know, etc.** Sound speech, appropriate to different characters and circumstances, and tending to spiritual good, requires much wisdom.

7-9. PERSONAL INFORMATION.

7. All my state (or, *affairs*) **shall Tychicus declare** (or, *make known*) **unto you.** Concerning Tychicus, see Acts 20 : 4; Eph. 6 : 21; 2 Tim. 4 : 12; Titus 3 : 12. He appears as one of the Asiatic companions of Paul on the third missionary journey, whether for all, or for only a part of the time, we cannot say. In the passage of Ephesians referred to he is spoken of in the same terms, and is sent upon the same mission as here. From what appears in the notices of him in 2 Timothy and Titus we find him faithfully tending upon the last labors of the aged and soon to be martyred apostle. Paul's language here is that of emphatic encomium. He is **beloved** as a brother, and **faithful** as a personal attendant (διάκονος), and a **fellow-servant**, or co-laborer (σύνδουλος) in the work of the Master.

8. Whom I have sent unto you for the same (or, *this very*) **purpose, that he might**

know your estate and comfort your hearts. The Revised Version reads: "That ye may know our [1] estate, and that he may comfort your hearts." Paul knew that they would be solicitous about him and thoughtfully sends them information and comfort.

9. With Onesimus—an escaped slave of Philemon, who had been converted at Rome under Paul's preaching and was now being returned to his master, bearing the letter addressed to Philemon. (See Epistle to Philemon.) **A faithful and beloved brother**—though an escaped slave and one who had been wicked. A good comment on 3 : 11 and 4 : 1. **Who is one of you.** From this it appears that Philemon was a Colossian. His relation to the church is suggested in the opening words of the letter addressed to him. (See Phil. 1.) **They shall make known all things that are done here.** There were many details concerning himself, his work, and the general state of affairs, which the Colossians would like to know, but which it was not necessary that he should write.

10-18. CONCLUDING SALUTATIONS.

10. Aristarchus, a Thessalonian, mentioned as a companion of Paul's work and sufferings in Acts 19 : 29; 20 : 4; 27 : 2; Philem. 24. On the expression **fellow-prisoner,** see especially Acts 27 : 2. On comparing our passage with Philem. 23, 24, it is noticed that while here Aristarchus is called "fellow-prisoner," Epaphras is called 'fellow-servant'; while in the Epistle to Philemon, Epaphras is called "fellow-prisoner" and Aristarchus is simply mentioned among the "fellow-workers." Meyer, and others after him, has deduced the plausible conjecture that these men *in turn and rot-*

---

[1] We have here an interesting variation. The question is whether to read ἵνα γνῷ τὰ περὶ ὑμῶν ('that he might know your estate') or ἵνα γνῶτε τὰ περὶ ἡμῶν ('that ye might know our estate'). The latter reading is found in A B D* F G P 10. 17. 33. 35. 37. 44. 47. 71. 111

116. 137., d e g, Armenian, Ethiopic, Euthalius, Theodoret, Jerome. It is preferred accordingly by Westcott and Hort, Tischendorf, Lightfoot, Meyer-Franke, and adopted by the Revisers.

11 And Jesus, which is called Justus, who are of the circumcision. These only *are my* fellow workers unto the kingdom of God, which have been a comfort unto me.

12 Epaphras, who is *one* of you, a servant of Christ, saluteth you, always labouring fervently for you in prayers, that ye may stand perfect and complete in all the will of God.

11 ceive him), and Jesus, who is called Justus, who are of the circumcision: these only *are my* fellow-workers unto the kingdom of God, men who have

12 been a comfort unto me. Epaphras, who is one of you, a [1] servant of Christ Jesus, saluteth you, always striving for you in his prayers, that ye may stand

---

1 Gr. *bondservant.*

---

untarily shared the apostle's prison, in order to be with him. This is rather a large inference. Paul may have called any one of his co-laborers who was by his side at the time a 'fellow-prisoner' without meaning that they were actually prisoners such as himself, or had become so voluntarily for his sake. Nor would it be necessary to suppose that these two alone took turns in the companionship and service of the apostle in his Roman imprisonment. **And Marcus.** See Acts 15: 37; 2 Tim. 4: 11. This is no doubt the "John Mark" of the Acts, the companion of Paul and Barnabas on their tour, who caused their separation by his defection, who was afterward forgiven by Paul, who later became the companion of Peter (1 Peter 5: 13), and the author of the second gospel. **Sister's son to Barnabas.** It is not positive whether the word means "nephew" (not necessarily 'sister's son'), or "cousin," being used in both senses. But Lightfoot has pretty clearly made out that "cousin" is the right rendering here, because "nephew" seems to be a late and inaccurate usage. This relationship, doubtless, helps to explain Barnabas' partiality for Mark in the memorable conflict with Paul regarding him.[1] **Touching whom ye received commandments.** Whose? and what? Commentators differ in their answers to these questions. It seems altogether most likely that the 'commandments' were Paul's own, and that the gist of them is found in the following words: **If he come unto you, receive him.** But this is not certain. They may have re-

ferred to something else. When, by whom, and for what purpose these 'commandments' had been sent does not appear. The whole passage goes to show that Paul had long ceased to feel any resentment about Mark's defection years ago, and did not wish him now to suffer in the esteem of others on that account.

11. Jesus, who is called Justus, is not elsewhere mentioned. **Who are of the circumcision.** Christian Jews, not Judaistic Christians. **These only are my fellow workers.** It is hard to understand the 'only' here. The interpretation preferred by Meyer, Lightfoot, and others, is that Paul means to say that these three were the only ones of the more prominent *Christian Jews* then at Rome, who were thoroughly in sympathy with him, and were a comfort to him in his work. From which it would follow that the others, even Luke, were not Jews. **Unto the kingdom of God**—that is, with a view to the kingdom, workers, together with him, for the bringing in of the kingdom. **Which have been a comfort to me.** The word (*παρηγορία*) comes from a verb meaning first "to address," then "to exhort," and then "to console." It became in the adjective form a medical term for soothing remedies, and so has come down to us as *paregoric!*

12. Epaphras, again. See note on 1 : 7, 8. **A servant of Christ.** Revised Version reads "Christ Jesus."[2] **Always labouring fervently for you in prayers**—as did also Paul himself. See 1: 3, 9, 29. **That ye may stand[2] perfect**—that is, fully-matured Christians.

---

[1] But Barnabas seems to have had a generous way of befriending those whom others thought to be wrong. He had acted so toward Paul himself on a very important and memorable occasion. Acts 9: 26, 27. This may partly explain his sympathy with Peter at Antioch (Ga 2: 13), when "Barnabas also was carried away with their dissimulation." This disposition may be a weakness, sometimes, as at Antioch; but it does not appear that Barnabas was wrong about Mark. Rather the contrary.

[2] The correct text adds Ἰησοῦ ('Jesus') after Χριστοῦ

("Christ"). Decisive. Westcott and Hort, Tischendorf, Lightfoot, Meyer-Franke all read σταθῆτε ('stand,' literally, "be made to stand," passive), instead of στῆτε ('stand,' active), with a few but weighty authorities against the multitude. They are probably correct, but the point is of no great importance. See exegetical note. More important is their reading, πεπληροφορημένοι ("completed" or "fully assured") for the common πεπληρωμένοι ("completed," "fulfilled"). Former is the reading of ℵ A B C D*, etc.

13 For I bear him record, that he hath a great zeal for you, and them *that are* in Laodicea, and them in Hierapolis.
14 Luke, the beloved physician, and Demas, greet you.
15 Salute the brethren which are in Laodicea, and Nymphas, and the church which is in his house.
16 And when this epistle is read among you, cause

13 perfect and fully assured in all the will of God. For I bear him witness, that he hath much labour for you, and for them in Laodicea, and for them in 14 Hierapolis. Luke, the beloved physician, and De-15 mas salute you. Salute the brethren that are in Laodicea, and [1] Nymphas, and the church that is in 16 [2] their house. And when [3] this epistle hath been

1 The Greek may represent *Nympha*. ....2 Some ancient authorities read *her*......3 Gr. *the*.

And complete.[1] Better to render, as in the Revised Version, " fully assured " ; that is, fully convinced in your minds of the truth. It *may* mean " fully completed," but the Revised Version rendering is better usage. **In all the will of God**—in all that God wills, his revealed truth, his declared precepts. This phrase goes either with "stand," and denotes the standing ground in which they come to maturity and full confidence, or it goes with these words themselves denoting the sphere (will of God) in which they arrive at maturity and confidence. It matters little; the general thought is the same in either case.

13. For I bear him record that he hath a great zeal for you (the Revised Version gives, " much labor[2] for you "). The 'labor' here refers more likely to the anxiety and prayer before mentioned (see on 1 : 7, 8); but it may be to his real outward exertions on their behalf. **And for them that are in Laodicea.** Laodicea was an important city in the Roman province of Asia, which was only a part of what is now called Asia Minor, or Turkey in Asia. It was not far from Colosse. No doubt the church, addressed later in the Book of Revelation as one of the "seven," was now in existence. **And for them in Hierapolis**—a city very near to Laodicea, noted for its warm springs. Thus the three cities were in the same neighbor-

hood, and the Christians residing in them naturally had much in common.

14. Luke, the beloved physician—the author of the third gospel and of the Acts, a faithful attendant upon Paul. See also 2 Tim. 4 : 10. **And Demas.** He afterward left the apostle (see 2 Tim. 4 : 10), and has been made by Bunyan the perpetual type of a deserter for money. From the fact that he is mentioned here without a word of praise while the others receive commendation in various ways, most interpreters have inferred that already his true character was beginning to appear, and that Paul did not have full confidence in him. This may be so, but Franke on Meyer wisely cautions against too sure an inference. See Philem. 24, where he is mentioned among the "fellow-workers."

15. Salute the brethren which are in Laodicea—as they could easily do, it being so near. **And Nymphas** (or, "Nympha"[3]). Not elsewhere mentioned, and it is not certain whether the person was a man or woman, as the form of the word in this case would be the same for both. **And the church which is in his** (or, *her*) **house.** I think "her" is most likely correct, and so that we should read "Nympha" above. She was probably a well-to-do woman, like Lydia, in whose house the church met. Compare Rom. 16 : 5; 1 Cor. 16 : 9.

16. And when this epistle is read among

1 See note 2, p. 54.
2 Tischendorf, Westcott and Hort, Lightfoot, Meyer-Franke, after ℵ A B C P 80. Euthalius, instead of ζῆλον ('zeal'), Received Text, or other variations found in various manuscripts.
3 Here is found a very interesting variation, though the point is of not much importance. It is whether to take Nymphas as a man's name, and read '*his* house,' or as a woman's name with "*her* house," or to take Nymphas and 'the brethren' together and read "*their* house." The authorities stand:
1. αὐτῶν ("their"). ℵ A C P 5. 9. 17. 23. 34. 39. 47. 73. Arabic, Euthalius.
2. αὐτοῦ ('his'). D E F G K L, most cursives, Coptic, Gothic; Chrysostom, Theodoret, Damascenus, and others.

3. αὐτῆς ("her"). B. 67.**
The Latin Versions are indecisive as between the second and third (ejus); so apparently also the Syriac. It is curious how our editors divide. Tischendorf, as might have been expected, follows ℵ, and reads the first; Westcott and Hort, as also might have been expected, follow B, and read the third; Lightfoot, who usually goes with Westcott and Hort after B, this time agrees with Tischendorf after ℵ, etc.; while, on the contrary, Meyer-Franke follows B and the English editors. It does not seem possible to decide positively between the first and third. We must, at all events, reject the second as a palpable correction. My own judgment inclines to the third, as it appears more likely that αὐτῶν would have grown out of αὐτῆς than *vice versa*. But see Lightfoot for the contrary opinion.

that it be read also in the church of the Laodiceans; and that ye likewise read the *epistle* from Laodicea. | read among you, cause that it be read also in the church of the Laodiceans; and that ye also read

---

you, etc. This interchange would be easy and natural from the nearness of the two places. Compare the injunction regarding the reading of the Epistle to the Thessalonians in 1 Thess. 5 : 27. It is possible that the objections which some would make to the contents of the letters made these earnest exhortations necessary. It is evident that a public reading before the congregation is meant. See also 1 Tim. 4 : 13, which may include the reading of the apostolic writings, as well as the Scriptures of the Old Testament. This is a suggestive hint as to the importance and authority of the apostolic writings in these earliest times **The epistle from Laodicea.** Interesting questions are brought up by this phrase: 1. What is meant by the peculiar form of the expression "*from* Laodicea"? Some say an epistle that the Laodiceans had written! Others, that it must be one that some other author had written 'from Laodicea.' Others, that it was one that Paul himself had written on some previous occasion 'from Laodicea.' But these are all useless attempts to explain what is clearly evident from the context: that it was an epistle written by Paul himself and addressed (probably at the same time) *to* Laodicea, which the Colossians were to procure *from* Laodicea that it might also be read in their church. This use of the preposition 'from' (*ἐκ*) is clearly paralleled in classical Greek and need occasion no difficulty. 2. If this explanation be accepted, the question comes up at once, what is the epistle to the Laodiceans? It is not extant under that name. To be sure, there *is* a Latin letter, so-called, but it is too clearly a forgery, made up of quotations from the various genuine epistles of Paul, to require notice here. See Lightfoot for a complete and able discussion of the matter. Leaving this out, we are still concerned to know what *is* the Epistle to Laodicea.

Two theories deserve notice: (1) That Paul did write by Tychicus at this time a letter to the Laodicean Church, and that it has been lost. The fact that it was not preserved is to be accounted for by the supposition that it was mainly occupied with matters of local and temporary interest, thus forming a sort of sup-

plement to the letter to the Colossians, making it proper that both should be read at both places, but not necessary that it should come down for the instruction of the churches in all time. But this labored explanation is not satisfactory. We find it hard to see how a letter regarded by the apostle himself as important, to be read at Colosse, though addressed to Laodicea—a letter no doubt (as all his letters are) full of valuable doctrine and precept; a letter addressed to a church in a larger and more important city than Colosse; a letter of Paul the apostle, all whose other letters to churches appear beyond doubt to be preserved for the church—we find it hard to see how such a letter could have been lost, *and no trace or mention of it recorded.* (2) Preference is accordingly given to the theory that the letter known to us as the Epistle to the Ephesians is the one here meant. The reasons for this are: (*a*) That the Epistle to the Ephesians has no personal salutations (which is very remarkable when we recall the apostle's long stay and wonderful work there), and thus may have been a circular letter, copies of which were sent to various churches. (*b*) That this view receives strange and striking confirmation from the decided doubt as to the genuineness of the words "in Ephesus" in the first verse of that Epistle. It seems probable that the place was left a blank, to be filled by the name of whatever church received a copy. (*c*) That the similarity of thought and style, and yet the differences due to circumstances; the teaching of one confirming the other, Colossians having a more special and local reference, Ephesians being more general; and the fact that both were sent by the hands of Tychicus and so apparently at the same time —all this serves to confirm the view adopted. These are the only two views that are worthy of choosing between. The question cannot be regarded as settled, but the weight of probability appears to me to be against the theory of a lost and unheard-of Epistle, and in favor of that which sees in the remarkable Epistle to the Ephesians a circular letter addressed to several churches, among others to that at Laodicea, and here directed to be read also at Colosse.

17 And say to Archippus, take heed to the ministry which thou hast received in the Lord, that thou fulfil it. 18 The salutation by the hand of me Paul. Remember my bonds. Grace be with you. Amen.

17 the epistle from Laodicea. And say to Archippus, Take heed to the ministry which thou hast received in the Lord, that thou fulfil it. 18 The salutation of me Paul with mine own hand. Remember my bonds. Grace be with you.

17. And say to Archippus—probably one of the pastors of the church at Colosse. See Philem. 2. Various speculations as to the person and work of Archippus have been put forth, but nothing further is even probably established than what has been said, that he was a pastor at Colosse. It may be, as Bengel acutely remarks, that the exhortation to fidelity in his office is addressed to him through the church for the sake of solemnity, that the church should be witness to this appeal. It does not imply censure, as some have supposed. **Take heed to the ministry.** As we might say, "Look well to the work of a pastor and teacher." **Which thou hast received in the Lord**—not only *from* the Lord, as a duty laid upon the recipient, but also '*in* the Lord,' as the solemn sphere of its reception and exercise. It is to the Lord that he must look for helpful grace in the performance of his work. **That thou fulfil it**—that is, fully perform its every duty.

18. Compare 1 Cor. 16 : 21; 2 Thess. 3 : 17. **The salutation by the hand of me Paul**—probably written in large and well-known characters. See Gal. 6 : 11. It seems that he had employed an amanuensis for the rest, but adds this last with his own hand, both as a seal of authenticity and as a matter of affectionate interest, which they might well appreciate. **Remember my bonds**—that is, especially in prayer. See above, ver. 3, 4. A pathetic ap-

peal, putting a personal emphasis on all he has written. Then follows the benediction, but in the shortest form. **Grace be with you.** God's favor in Christ be upon you. The **amen** is to be omitted.[1]

HOMILETICAL SUGGESTIONS.

Ver. 2: Three characteristics of prayer: Continuance, watchfulness, and thankfulness. **Ver. 3:** Preacher's need of the prayers of his people for enlarged opportunity—more people to preach to, and more power in preaching to them. **Ver. 4:** Clear and fearless preaching always needed. **Ver. 5:** 1. The outer circle —community, congregation, home. 2. Wise demeanor toward them—need, power, source of this wisdom. 3. Use of opportunities in the work—the phrase and its application. **Ver. 6:** Three elements of prudent speech: agreeable, pointed, appropriate. **Ver. 7:** Tychicus an example of those suggestive characters that are only slightly mentioned in the Scripture. See the notes. **Ver. 8, 9:** The instructive mutual solicitude of Paul and the Colossians. **Ver. 15:** Little known of these, but that little is much—a church in the house! **Ver. 17:** The minister and his ministry: 1. The personal element—'say to Archippus.' 2. The care needed—'take heed.' 3. Sacredness of the trust—'in the Lord.' 4. Magnitude of the work—'that thou fulfil it.'

[1] 'Ἀμήν ('amen') is to be omitted on decisive authority: ℵ A B C, etc. The postscript it rightly omitted by all modern critics. It was evidently added by later hands, and appears in the manuscripts in various forms.

www.ingramcontent.com/pod-product-compliance
Lightning Source LLC
Chambersburg PA
CBHW031750090426
42739CB00008B/958